D1544263

Sasha Cohen

FIRE
ON ICE

Sasha Cohen

WITH AMANDA MACIEL

FIRE ON ICE

AUTOBIOGRAPHY OF A
CHAMPION FIGURE SKATER

PHOTOGRAPHS BY
KATHY GOEDEKEN

HarperCollinsPublishers

Sasha Cohen: Fire on Ice

Photos on pages 1–9, 13, 15, 17, 25, 31, 32, 60, 80, 97, 103, 104, 114,
151, 153, 154, and 155 courtesy of the Cohen family
Photos on pages XII, XV, 41, 43, 44, 51, 53, 54, 75, 84, 89, 108, 111,
113, 115, 117, 120, 132, 137, 141, 142, 144, 147, 148, 150, 152, 161, 167,
169, and 170 copyright © Kathy Goedeken
Color photos on insert pages 1, 2, 3, and 4 (top) courtesy of
the Cohen family
Color photos on insert pages 4 (bottom) and 6–16
copyright © Kathy Goedeken

Library of Congress Cataloging-in-Publication Data
Cohen, Sasha
Fire on ice : autobiography of a champion figure skater / Sasha
Cohen with Amanda Maciel ; photographs by Kathy Goedeken.—
1st Avon ed.
   p.   cm.
ISBN 0-06-072489-7 (pbk.) — ISBN 0-06-072490-0
1. Cohen, Sasha, 1984- —Juvenile literature. 2. Skaters—United
States—Biography—Juvenile literature. 3. Women skaters—
United States—Biography—Juvenile literature. I. Maciel,
Amanda. II. Goedeken, Kathy, ill. III. Title.
GV850.C65A3   2005   2004021618
796.91'2'092—dc22

Typography by Karin Paprocki
1 2 3 4 5 6 7 8 9 10
❖
First Edition

Dedication

TO EVERYONE WHO'S BEEN A PART OF MY AMAZING roller-coaster ride, helping me out and being there to guide and inspire me. But especially to my mom, who's always been there every step of the way. For not being a crazy skating mom, but a pillar of support.

Of course, I would be nothing without my amazing family. I love you so much—Daddy, Natasha, Babba, Grandma, Grandpa.

Acknowledgments

TO THE PEOPLE WHO MADE IT HAPPEN: LINDA Stiegler and Kathy Stafford, for inspiring me to write this book; Amanda Maciel and Abby McAden, for making this project come together so wonderfully; and Kathy Goedeken, for capturing so many moments of my life along the way.

Contents

Sasha Cohen

FIRE
ON ICE

✳ *At the 2002 Winter Olympics*

Introduction

FEBRUARY 2002

I WALK INTO THE LOCKER ROOM, THE LAST IN MY group of six skaters to come in. The other girls are already changing, touching up their makeup, and nervously getting ready to take the ice for the first time at the Olympics in Salt Lake City. I've been warming up until the last minute, trying to keep my muscles warm and ready for the most important short program of my career so far.

Everyone is nervous, keeping to themselves. I open my skate bag, take out my tights, dress, and skates, and start getting ready. A skater who's just finished her program comes in, carrying stuffed animals and flowers and looking relieved. We gaze at her with envy. The worst part is the waiting.

An Olympic official sticks her head in the door and says, "We need you in five minutes! Do you need anything? Are you ready?"

I quickly adjust my dress, touch up my lip gloss, and

I'm ready to go, but I still have to wait. I walk to the backstage area and nervously pace behind the blue curtain, keeping warm as I hear the last skater's program music come to an end. All six of us are by the barrier now, anxious for the skater's marks to be announced so we can step onto the ice.

I've been to this arena before for practice sessions. But today is completely different. There's not a space that's not filled with people. Coaches, cameramen, commentators, judges, fans. The Olympic rings, painted everywhere, are huge. There's tons of noise—practice is always quiet, and this is the exact opposite. The whole world is here.

Finally they announce our warm-up group. The six of us rush forward, trying to be the first onto the ice. I talk myself through my routine as a burst of applause comes from the audience. I start to feel better, more in control. They clap for us, and especially for me, the only American in the group—the fans in Salt Lake City are incredibly supportive of all the athletes on the U.S. team.

I take my usual approach, methodically talking myself through everything: okay, just breathe, step, spin, crossover, keep going, warm up this jump, this landing, hold, balance. I'm trying not to overwhelm myself. It's so easy to slip into, *Oh my God, look at all these people. Oh my God, I'm at the Olympics!*

But I keep my mind on what I'm doing; I keep breathing.

With about a minute left, I've warmed up all my elements. I slowly skate around the rink, resting and calming my nerves. I'll be the first skater in the warm-up group to perform.

I keep my legs going, then stop at the boards near my coach. After retying my skates and adjusting my dress, I have one last talk with my coach, John Nicks.

This is his tenth trip to the Games, so I'm ready for some magical Olympic knowledge. Mr. Nicks is the calmest person in the world. I may be jittery, but, as always, he is steady and reassuring. He smiles, takes my hands, and just says, "Good luck, dear."

Thirty seconds later, a booming voice from the loudspeaker announces, "From the United States of America, Sasha Cohen!"

I feel a big rush inside me when they call my name. The audience applauds as I skate to the center of the ice.

✳ *Me and Mr. Nicks practicing at the Olympics in Salt Lake City*

As the applause fades, I tell myself, *Okay, this is it. You're at the Olympics. This is your chance—take it!*

I stop and hit my opening position and think, *You can do this.*

And then I take a deep breath, and the music begins.

Chapter One

GYMNASTICS AND ICE CREAM
1984 TO 1991

THE STORY OF MY LIFE BEGINS WITH MY FAMILY. I'm really close to my parents, my grandparents, and my little sister, Natasha. They've all been a huge support to me throughout my career, and when I'm not on the ice, we just have fun. We travel a lot, and during the holidays we all cook together. When I'm at home, we don't talk about skating—it's just us.

My mom, Galina, was born in Odessa, Ukraine. Like a lot of Russian children, my mom was trained in both gymnastics and ballet. She wanted to ice skate, but the rink was under construction

for ten years and she never got a chance. Mom came to America and learned English quickly, then studied at San Diego State University and UC Berkeley. She then went on to study business at UCLA. I was born within two years and ten blocks of where she graduated.

My dad, Roger, was raised in Palo Alto, near San Francisco. He was a great skier and spent two years studying at the American College of Switzerland in a ski resort. After studying European history for two years, he attended UC San Diego and UC Berkeley Law School. While studying abroad he learned to cook, and we love trying new restaurants together.

My parents met in San Diego, while they were both in college. My dad asked my mom out on a date the first time they met. He proposed within three months, and they were married within a year.

I was born at UCLA Hospital on October 26, 1984.

My mom says I was a robust, bright-eyed, and energetic newborn. They named me Alexandra Pauline Cohen. I almost always go by Sasha, a common Russian nickname for Alexandra—and a much easier word to handle when I was little and learning to write.

Soon after I was born, my parents moved to Pasadena. We were happy there, and when I was almost four years old, more happiness arrived: my little sister.

On June 28, 1988, Natalia Zina-ida Cohen was born, also at UCLA hospital. My parents nicknamed her Natasha. I thought of her as my new toy. My earliest memory of her

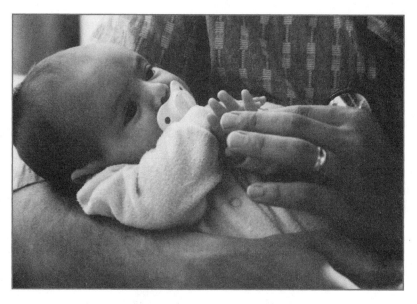

✳ *My brand-new baby sister, Natasha*

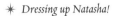

is of sticking little gift bows on her head.

One Christmas I got a nurse's outfit that included a toy stethoscope, thermo-meter, and plastic syringe. Natasha was my favorite patient. I put the ther-mometer in her mouth and poked the plastic syringe into her arm. In our family photo album is a picture of me in my nurse's outfit—grinning from ear to ear—and Natasha struggling to escape her treatment.

Pretty soon after Natasha was born, my mom decided to quit her job in international banking to stay home with us. I loved having her around, especially the day of my first earthquake.

I was playing under our dining room table when the room began to shake and rumble. I didn't know what was happening, but as soon as everything stopped shaking, I crawled out from under the table and said, "I am so sorry, Mommy. I won't ever do that again!"

Of course my mom explained that it wasn't my fault.

But by that time I'd already had a lot of experience with being in trouble, and a lot of "time-outs." Usually when I was given a time-out, my response was, "I will be *so* good next time."

Once I even tried to negotiate my punishment. My dad was tucking me under his arm and carrying me to my room, and I looked him in the eye and said, "Dad, before my time-out, I want ten candies."

He said, "No, Sasha. You are being punished. You can't have any candies."

"Okay, five candies?" I countered.

"No, Sasha. *No* candies."

"Three candies?" I cried.

"None," my dad said.

As he put me down in my room and started to close the door, I said, "Okay, Dad, my final offer: Give me one candy, and I'll take a lick and spit it out." My dad

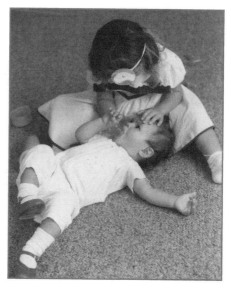

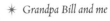
✳ *Grandpa Bill and me*

laughed so hard, he almost let me out of my time-out early.

Natasha and I loved visiting my dad's family near San Francisco. My grandma's house is unique for all its arts and crafts, which she collects in her travels around the world. Sometimes I think she might need a bigger house for all the artwork she's collected.

My grandma has the best recipe for oatmeal–chocolate chip cookies. She taught us how to measure and mix the ingredients so we could help bake them when we visited. She also let us eat lots of dough.

My mother's parents are also very special to

✳ *Grandma Katcya, me, and Mom*

Natasha and me. They introduced us to Russian culture. We call them Babba and Dyed, which are the Russian names for "Grandma" and "Grandpa." They had a comfortable home in San Diego with a swimming pool, which we loved playing in.

Dyed is the best at barbecuing chicken—perfect for dinner on warm summer afternoons with a big group of my mom's relatives around the table. After dinner, Natasha would play the piano for all of us.

Babba always cooks up a storm and insists that we "Eat, eat, eat!"—like any good Russian grandma. That's always been an easy order to follow, especially when she makes one of her delicious cakes. Our favorite is the "flourless" cake, made from ground walnuts, eggs, sugar, and lots of butter. It's so good, we usually polish it off in one sitting. (I have a copy of the recipe posted on my Web site, www.sashacohen.com, if you want to try it!)

With all my determination and her grandmotherly

✳ Every year for generations, my father's family has met for vacations in Central Camp, near Yosemite.

soft spot, Babba had a hard time disciplining me. I remember her saying, "Sasha, you cannot have ice cream if you do not finish your doughnut first!" And she had this great rule: We couldn't have ice cream more than three times a day. Natasha and I took full advantage of this. Our parents didn't let us have junk food at home, so when Babba and Dyed took us to the candy store, we'd clean the place out.

By the time I turned four, I was tearing up the house,

jumping on everything, a bundle of energy. My mom and my grandfather had both done gymnastics—in fact, Dyed had once performed in a big parade in Moscow for Joseph Stalin—and my mom thought a class or two would be a good way to wear me out and keep me from destroying the house.

So I started at Flair's gym, three or four hours a week. It was really intense training. We were all around five years old, already doing hours of serious training. We did the floor, beam, vault, and the uneven parallel bars. My favorite was the trampoline. The coaches had to drag me off it when we went through all the exercises. I'd stay on it until one of the coaches would say sternly, "Okay, Sasha, you have to rotate now."

I also remember a huge pit in the gym, filled with foam cubes. Sometimes at the end of our workouts the coaches would let us

✴ *My days as a gymnast*

jump in, and they'd throw in a prize, like a necklace or a key chain. The eight of us would scramble through the foam, which was pretty deep, especially for little kids. One time I saw the necklace and took off after it, but another girl got there one second before me. I was *so* disappointed to lose—my competitive spirit kicked in pretty early, I guess.

When I was six I competed on the gym's team. I only placed fourth or fifth, but it was good practice. After one competition I went into the storeroom and saw all the extra trophies. I'd won a few little ones, but these were gigantic, almost as tall as I was. "Do you think they'd mind if I took one? They have so many," I said to my mom. I guess I didn't fully understand what competitions were about, and I didn't know anything about the Olympics. But I definitely wanted a big trophy!

When I wasn't practicing gymnastics, I was playing at home with my friends and spending time with my family. My grandparents in San Diego would take Natasha and me to Seaport Village, a cute shopping center on the bay. We'd walk along the promenade, chase birds, climb trees, watch the performers, ride on the carousel, and get glittery unicorns painted on our cheeks.

Most importantly, we'd get ice cream. My parents let me have ice cream on each trip to Seaport Village, but they limited me to one scoop. Even then I liked to try a lot of different flavors, but I couldn't pick a favorite. I was too short to see into the freezer, so my dad would lift me up and I'd peer in at all the flavors, usually sampling as many as possible before deciding on one.

When I was five, my parents would only buy me a kid-size cone (of course). So one time, up on the freezer display, I told the salesperson, "Please make my kid's cone extra large." He laughed and gave me a huge scoop.

Another time, we were at a restaurant at the beach and I'd ordered ice cream in a cup—but they forgot to bring me a spoon. Undaunted, I walked over to the shelf that held all the utensils, a big plastic container of forks, knives, and spoons. It was much taller than I was, so I stood on tiptoe, grabbed the edge of the container, and pulled it slowly toward me to see where the spoons were. I found one and grabbed it, as the rest of the silverware fell out, with a huge, loud clatter, onto the floor around me.

The restaurant went silent.

I held up my spoon and cried, "I got it!" Everyone laughed and started applauding. I was little, but I was very determined!

Unfortunately, when it came to gymnastics, I wasn't nearly as focused as I was with ice cream. I was all over the place, easily excited and distracted. I didn't have the maturity to handle the advanced tricks I was learning. By the time I was seven, I was practicing three hours a day and taking private lessons, doing dangerous elements, so it was crucial to be precise. For example, one day I was doing a back handspring series and I didn't notice the four-inch beam near me on the floor. By sheer luck I sprang over it, but if my timing had been off at all, I would have smashed my head. At that age, I just didn't have the right mind-set to handle my workouts safely.

My mom was in the stands watching me, as always, and saw my near-miss. Gymnastics used up all my energy, but she could see I wasn't very aware, and obviously it was time for a change. Sitting next to her was my friend Allison Larson's grandmother, Sally. Sally told my mom that, in addition to gymnastics, Allison ice skated, and suggested I try it, too. My mom liked the idea.

And that's really where it all began.

Chapter Two

ON THE ICE
1991 TO 1993

FROM THE SECOND I HIT THE ICE, I LOVED SKATING.
I skated as fast as I could, loving the speed, the wind in my

face. I'd fly across the ice, fall, laugh, get up, and do it all over again—and again. Gymnastics was soon forgotten, and skating became my new passion.

I knew that first day that I wanted to learn more. The cold, the feeling of being out of control, and the bumps and bruises from falling on the ice didn't bother me. I begged my mom to sign me up for group lessons. Before I had even removed those worn-out rental skates, I was hooked.

Of course, when I asked my mom to enroll me in lessons, I never realized the commitment that my whole family would be making. After a few weeks of lessons, the other moms were warning mine that she'd soon be taking me to the rink for 5:30 A.M. practices. She told them that would never happen. My mom's a very energetic person, but she likes taking her time in the mornings, enjoying her latte.

And, luckily for both of us, my mom was right: I never had to skate before 7:45 in the morning. But the ice-skating moms were also right—at least partly: My mom was taking me to the rink a lot more often.

I couldn't wait to get on the ice every time. My skating friends and I would bring music and create our own programs and play around, creating new moves.

My family has never watched much TV, but I do remember watching Kristi Yamaguchi in the 1992 Olympics. I had a poster of her on my wall for years. I used to watch a tape of that Olympics, with Kristi, Midori Ito, and Nancy Kerrigan. I guess I didn't realize it was a

✳ Praying for a medal—literally

tape—I thought I was watching a new competition each time, and I remember being so impressed that Kristi won so many gold medals. I had a few little medals of my own on my bedroom wall, and I remember thinking, *Kristi's wall must be* covered *with gold medals by now!*

But I didn't rush to be too competitive too soon. I made steady progress in learning the basics, and I also learned a lot by having fun on the ice.

After moving through my beginning, or Pre-Alpha-level lessons, I signed up for classes with Darlene Sparks

Bell. Darlene had competed as a skater at the Nationals level and was trained by Carlo Fassi, who, with his wife, Christa, had coached a long line of great skaters, including Olympic gold medalists Robin Cousins, Dorothy Hamill, and Peggy Fleming.

Darlene believed in me from the very beginning. She told my mom I had potential and encouraged her to sign me up for more lessons. To this day, I can always call Darlene for advice or encouragement. As a coach, she was always energetic and made class really fun.

In my group lessons I'd spend a lot of time looking around the rink to see what the more advanced skaters were learning. While I was learning swizzles, waltz jumps, and two-foot spins, my mind was calculating how quickly I could move on to what the "big girls" were doing. So it was thrilling when I completed the group lessons and my mom put me into my first private classes.

Mom chose a coach at our rink who had competitive experience. His name was Victor Yelchin. He was from Russia, where he'd skated at the championship level and later starred in ice tours.

During my lessons and practices, my mom had dressed me in thick tights and a stretchy skirt that went down to my knees. It was a warm outfit, but Victor was appalled. "This isn't a skating dress!" he told us. "The skirt is too long! She'll trip. It's time to get a real skating dress."

That was good news to me—I've always loved shopping for clothes. That same day, Mom and I went to the rink's pro shop to pick out my first real skating outfit. We looked through everything and selected a dress with a stretchy turquoise fabric and a gold pattern. The dress had three layers of skirts, very very flouncey. I *loved* it.

✴ *Natasha always thought ice skating was too cold, but I got her out there once in a while.*

Then it was time to buy skates so I could stop killing my feet in rentals. When they brought over my boots, my mom protested, "Wait, these don't have blades!"

"They all come that way," the salesperson explained. "The blades are sold separately."

But my mom still wasn't sure. After the salesman opened several other boxes of boots to show us—none of them had blades attached—she had to believe him.

Finally I had my own coach, boots, blades, and fancy skating dress. I was ready for the next level.

We started to learn about the different levels of skating and how to progress through them. Competition begins for skaters as early as age three, but the levels of competition are based on skill rather than age. By the time I started training with Victor I was eleven and at the juvenile level.

I competed a few times with Victor. He cut my first program, using music from the opera *Carmen*. It was about a minute and a half long, with a few spins, jumps, and a couple of spirals. I don't remember the program, but I definitely remember going to competitions. I liked looking at what the other girls were wearing, how they did their hair and makeup. I liked that I got to wear my mom's makeup, even if it was only for competitions. I remember her applying lipstick and tightly pulling my hair into a neat ponytail, then blasting it with Paul Mitchell hairspray. The smell of that hairspray and the taste of a certain lipstick still make me nervous.

My mom always went to my competitions, and Dad and Natasha came to watch important events. A competition would be an all-day event: I'd compete, then stay to watch how the other girls did. There were always vendors at the rinks, selling skating outfits and skating-related stuff. Babba and Dyed would come to my events and would always buy me something afterward, a doll or something fun. Then I'd play with all the girls that were finished competing—all of us in sweatpants but still wearing our perfect hair and makeup, running around to the video arcade and the snack bar. At the end of the night we'd all go out for dinner with our moms. I remember having fun more clearly than I remember actually competing.

But there was also a lot of frustration, especially because the other skaters had a huge lead in their skills. Most of my competitors started skating at age four or five, while I'd been seven in my first group classes. They were completing double jumps while I was struggling to master my singles.

By the time I left our rink in Pasadena, I had mastered

my waltz jump. It's the simplest of all the jumps, creating the foundation for all the others. And I'd also laid a foundation for my next big step. I didn't realize it then, but we were about to move to another city, and I would be moving to the ice rink of the famous Mr. Nicks, in Costa Mesa, California.

Chapter Three

NEW HOUSE, NEW COACHES
1993 TO 1997

WE MOVED TO ORANGE COUNTY, KNOWN AS "THE O.C.," in 1993, when I was eight years old. Natasha and I were excited about the move, though of course we were also sad to leave our friends and schools in Pasadena. For the first year or so we rented a house while my mom designed and oversaw the building of our new home in Laguna Niguel.

Mom worked with an architect to design the house, and she picked out all the interior elements herself. I remember us driving around to pick out faucets, the refrigerator, tiles. When we moved in we were amazed—a big, brand-new house, custom-designed for us. It was beautiful, located on top of a mountain overlooking a canyon and the ocean.

Meanwhile, I found a new rink, the Ice Capades Chalet,

The architect's drawing of our new house in Laguna Niguel

in Costa Mesa. Famous for being the home of coach John Nicks, the rink was the training ground for his world-class students, including champion pairs skaters Todd Sand and Jenni Meno.

I started taking lessons with Mr. Nicks's wife, Yvonne. She was the official spin coach of the rink. Gymnastics had made me very flexible, and I've continued to stretch throughout my years of skating. Working with her was a great experience, and I continued to take weekly spin lessons from her as long as I trained in California.

Yvonne Nicks took me to my first United States Figure Skating Association (USFSA) competition. I was still learning my jumps, and we were both pleasantly surprised when I skated well and placed second.

Things get more serious when you reach the juvenile level, but you're still pretty much on your own. My coaches weren't supervising me outside my twice weekly private lessons. My mom and I had to figure a lot out, and there's a lot to know. Skates alone are confusing—there are more than twenty different kinds of boots, fifteen kinds of blades. And I didn't know anything about off-ice training.

I did a lot of watching and learning, my mom and I doing extra work on our own. We drove around, to San Diego or Lake Arrowhead or Paramount, to work with different coaches on different jumps and elements.

Finding quality ice on a rink that wasn't super crowded or offering sessions at terrible times was also a challenge. We probably went to every rink in Southern California, but my favorite was the Ice Castle International Training Center, in Lake Arrowhead, a small, beautiful, mountain-top town. I especially remember visiting the pet store at Lake Arrowhead every time we were there. I'd always beg my mom for a kitten, and finally, on my eleventh birthday, she relented and we brought home Meow Meow. About a year later, Natasha convinced our parents to get her a cute, small dog. That's how a Pomeranian named Mocha joined the family.

Tons of elite athletes train at Ice Castle. I remember

seeing Michelle Kwan train there for the Olympics in 1998. Skaters from all over the world would practice there, and it was so inspiring to watch them and practice on the same ice they were skating on.

After Yvonne Nicks, I trained with Barbara Brown. Together we made a lot of progress, making me a better competitor and a stronger skater, especially as I started to learn my double jumps. Later I would get my single axel while working with her. I remember falling a lot, and always trying to catch up with the other kids. I would just go around and around, soaking wet from falling so much, trying to master that jump.

I also took lessons from Roger Bass, the "official" technical coach of the rink, who helped me master my combination jumps.

My first big competition was in November 1996, the Southwest Pacific Regionals, a huge event for which I'd need a new costume. A friend of my grandmother makes dresses, so we went to see her.

Of course, my mom and I had no experience in what makes a good skating dress, so when we went to the fabric store we just picked the most beautiful fabrics we could find, something that would look Spanish: red satin and black chiffon; gold lace; black textured velvet. To us, this seemed like the makings of Carmen. We brought them all to the designer, and she made an amazing dress with something like six skirts and these really big sleeves. I thought it was so pretty.

The judges at the critique session, which was held before the competition, told me not to wear it because there was just too much fabric for my little body. Once we found out that I'd be judged by different people at the actual competition, I wore it, anyway—and discovered firsthand why they had told me not to: The materials didn't stretch, the sleeves made it hard to move my arms, there were so many skirts. . . . It was definitely a good

✳ *Me and Naomi Nari Nam in our supercool "Why Be Normal?" sweatshirts, which we loved and wore everywhere at Sectionals in Salt Lake City*

lesson in how to make a competitive skating dress!

Because there are so many girls competing at the juvenile level at Regionals, four or five qualifying rounds are held. I skated better than anyone expected, and made it to the final round. Then I placed fourth, and it was so satisfying to defy everyone's expectations at my first big event! At that level, you medal if you're in the top four. I got to stand on the podium with my own medal and flowers, and it was so exciting. I loved it up there.

That same year, I started taking lessons from Mr. Nicks. A few months later, we asked if he would be my full-time coach. I had moved up to the intermediate level, and it was an honor that he accepted me as his student.

Every time I had a lesson with Mr. Nicks, I was really nervous. I felt I had to do everything perfectly. Despite my jitters, I was so inspired. Practicing with him was like a competition. Mr. Nicks was used to coaching older, more advanced skaters, and I was so in awe of him. I wanted him to think I was really good.

One of his other students was Naomi Nari Nam, who became a friend and competitor of mine. She was about my age, but much more advanced than I was—everyone was!—and I learned a lot from watching her.

When I first went to the Costa Mesa rink, I was sort of

known as the little wild girl who was out of control and would fall on everything. Everyone had their double jumps, and I didn't even have my single axel. As I moved closer to their level, I started becoming friends with the more advanced girls. Naomi and I began to get more competitive later on, and watching each other skate always pushed us to be better, to get to the next level.

That season I went to the Southwest Pacific Regionals again, this time as an intermediate skater. I placed second and qualified for the Pacific Coast Sectionals for the first time—a very big deal, a huge step forward, and a very exciting trip to my first competition outside Southern California.

I flew into Salt Lake City for Sectionals, barely able to contain my excitement. My friend Tiffany Stiegler was there, too, competing in pairs with her brother Johnnie, and over the next week we became really close friends. A lot of other people I knew were all there, and it was so exciting that I'd made it so far, competing with all these new skaters.

Competitions can be a lot of fun, especially those that require you to travel and stay in a hotel. When you check in, they give you a goody bag filled with gear or snacks or other fun stuff. You get to see girls you've heard of but have never seen skate, and watching them for the first time is so interesting and stimulating.

I don't remember the actual competition at Sectionals as well as I remember being thrilled to be in a new city with all the excitement of a big event. But I skated well enough to place fourth, which qualified me for the Junior Olympics in Anaheim.

Junior Olympics were an even bigger deal, but for me it didn't feel quite as special, because it was being held so close to my hometown. I stayed home, and didn't get the full hotel experience. And my frustrations about being technically behind the other skaters were worse. Mr. Nicks took me to the official practice session on the competition ice before the event, and I could see that all the other girls—or most of them, anyway—had already mastered their double axels and a triple jump. Seeing how upset I was, Mr. Nicks told me, "Maybe you should just practice at our rink until the competition starts." So I did. Being on my own ice kept me more focused, and I wasn't able to look around and worry about what jumps everyone else was landing.

At Nationals I was the last to compete in the long program. I got ready in the rink's bathroom, my mom helping me, as usual, with dressing, makeup, hair braiding, and hairspray. My whole family was there to watch me, and being close to home suddenly felt really nice.

I was still nervous, of course. I wanted to medal so badly, and I knew I wouldn't get to go to the North American challenge if I didn't. But the girls ahead of me were a lot more advanced, so when I placed fifth, I was content.

The next day I went back to middle school, took a week off, and started training for the next season, even more determined to master my jumps and catch up to my competition—and pass them.

Chapter Four

TRAINING FOR THE NEXT LEVEL
1997 TO 1999

IN THE SUMMER OF 1997, WHEN I WAS 12, I SPENT A lot more time training in Lake Arrowhead. My friend Allison Larson from Pasadena had moved there, and I'd go up and spend the weekend with her, watching the elite session at the rink on Friday nights and then going out for Chinese food with skater friends Robin Morris and Tiffany Stiegler. I'd train on Saturday mornings, and then Saturday afternoons we'd ride out on the Stiegler family's boat to water ski, or take lessons from the cute older boys who taught there. And sometimes for Saturday brunch we went to the Belgian Waffle House, my favorite place of all. The first time we went I was amazed to see chocolate chip waffles with ice cream on the menu. What a great idea! As always, my mom was the voice of reason when I tried to order them. "No, Sasha, you can't have that for breakfast."

＊ *Me, Robin Morris, and Tiffany Stiegler at the Chinese restaurant at Lake Arrowhead*

At the rink I took lessons from Russian pairs coach Irina Rodnina. She worked with me a lot on my jumps and stroking. I also worked with Elena Tcherkasskaia, a Russian prima ballerina with the Bolshoi Ballet who taught ballet choreography and emotion on the ice.

I practiced all this back in Costa Mesa, too, and the sides of my hips were covered with bruises from trying to land my double axel. I would go full-speed, try to complete the two and a half rotations, and usually fall, sliding halfway down the rink on my hip—needless to say, I was completely black and blue.

✳ *Elena Tcherkasskaia training me at the Lake Arrowhead rink*

One day I noticed that one of the girls from a pairs team had padded shorts on. This was an even better idea than chocolate-chip waffles for breakfast—I had to get some. The pairs skater helped me track them down, and falling was a lot less painful after that.

Around that time I had a pretty bad accident. I was on an empty practice session in Costa Mesa, the only skater on the ice besides one other girl, another top skater. I was stretching my leg out at the end of a landing while she was doing a jump and we completely didn't see each other—until she landed into my right calf with her blade. At first I wasn't sure anything was wrong. I was kind of shocked, but my tights weren't even ripped, so I took a careful lap around the ice. My leg definitely didn't feel right. I got off, sat on the bench, and pulled my tights up—and noticed blood. I ran up to the pro shop to change out of my tights completely, and Jenni Meno came in. I'm really squeamish and I was starting to panic. "It's okay, you're fine, it's gonna be fine," Jenni told me.

Then Naomi walked in, and she completely lost it. "Oh my GOD!" she yelled. "What happened? There's a huge hole in your leg!" Jenni immediately sent her out of the room.

My mom had just left the rink a half hour earlier, called home to be with Natasha, who had a 104-degree fever and needed to be taken care of at home. My dad came to pick me up and took me to the hospital, where they gave me twenty-one stitches, ten on the outside of my calf and eleven on the inside. In the end I was really, really lucky—the gash had just missed my muscle and the injury healed pretty quickly. I only had to take a few weeks off from skating.

By the end of the summer, I was getting closer to landing my double axel. I was also going into the eighth grade, and that was the year we decided I would stop going to my regular school. I switched to Futures High School, a special school that allows athletes and artists a schedule with enough flexibility to attend school and pursue their career at the same time. I still had plenty of homework and classes, but I was able to spend a big part of my day at the rink, and still go home in the afternoons around the same time Natasha got home from school. She and I bickered a lot then—"Give me back my sweater," "Stay out of my room," stuff like that—but looking back I'm glad I was able to be home with her, instead of spending my whole day at school and the rink. And of course, it was nice to still not need to get up too early in the morning for practice!

The double axel is a daunting jump, because you don't

really know if you're ever going to be able to learn it. Most skaters quit because they can never get their double axel. It's the glass ceiling, the major line. Once you have it, you kind of establish yourself as a skater. If you don't, you can't compete at the upper levels.

I practiced it a lot, and started to land, then cheated—landing and then turning, instead of rotating in the air and landing backward. It felt *almost* right, but it wasn't quite there. I've always learned my jumps by double-footing them at first—landing on two feet instead of one—especially that one. My left blade hit the tip of my right boot so many times, I eventually sliced the toe of the boot right off.

That October I finally got it. It was the most amazing rush. Whenever I landed it, I wanted to do it over and over again. And I did—I practiced it endlessly. It was just incredible, the biggest sense of accomplishment and the best feeling.

By that time, Regionals was just two weeks away. I had also landed my triple Salchow just a week before. Finally I had moved up to the competitive level of the girls my age. I was just around the corner from my thirteenth birthday.

Mr. Nicks had decided I was ready to move up to the novice level. Moving up a level requires taking a test, performing a new long program with that level's required elements. The test is actually a lot easier than what you need to be competitive. But novice is a big move, because at that point you can qualify to compete in the U.S. Nationals, known as the "big" Nationals.

I've always loved how skating presents new challenges, new goals, one after another. I try to focus on the next big competition as I move forward, rather than dreaming of the Olympics all the time. Making it to Nationals became my next goal.

That year I placed second at Regionals and at Sectionals. I landed my first double axel and triple jump in competition at Regionals, and my placement at Sectionals sent me on to my goal.

Being a Novice at Nationals is the best. It was a really eye-opening experience for me, seeing skaters from all over the country, being in that environment with the top competitors. I was thrilled to go into the skater's lounge and see all the skaters I'd watched on television and admired. I remember running to my mom to tell her, "I just saw Tara Lipinski!"

I was so excited to be there, but my short program was disappointing. I made one costly mistake, stepping out of a combination in the beginning. I was ranked sixth going into the long, and then I made a few mistakes in that program, too. Overall I placed sixth and I took it pretty hard. I shed a good amount of tears that night, spent a couple days wishing I could do it over. Then I moved on and had fun.

The novice competition ended early in the week, and tons of my friends were there. I put my mistakes behind me and concentrated on the next big thing—having a blast for the rest of the week. We toured Philadelphia, watched the other skaters compete, and ran around like crazy. For the competitor's party I had bought a beautiful, long, beaded black dress. At the arena, during the senior ladies long programs, we stopped to get ice cream cones, and we were jumping around, laughing. I decided, in the moment, to do a high kick—which was completely impossible in that long dress! My leg went up and the rest of me went down, flat on my back. The other girls were screaming laughing, especially Tiffany. I just remember lying on the floor, still holding up my empty ice cream cone—with all the ice cream now on my shoulder. So embarrassing!

One month after we got back home the 1998 Olympics started. Everyone at Costa Mesa was glued to the TV, to see Jenni and Todd compete in the pairs skating. It was the most important competition I had watched up till then, the most exciting time. The whole rink was buzzing, thrilled and nervous for them.

I trained on my own for a week, since Mr. Nicks had gone to Japan with them. Jenni and Todd didn't medal there, but they went on to win silver at the World Championships a few weeks later. Before they left, Todd was having a lot of problems with his triple toe. I had just learned the jump myself, and we practiced a little bit together. I gave him what advice I could, and he actually called me right after his short program at Worlds to say, "I remembered what you told me, and I landed it!" I went around for weeks telling people, "I helped Todd Sand with his triple toe at Worlds!"

It was the end of another season, and time to prepare for my test to move up to the junior level. I had qualified for the North American Challenge in Lake Placid, New York, taking place in July, and by the time I got there I was skating as a junior.

In the meantime I did my usual summer work, training new elements on the ice, listening to CDs with my mom, picking music out for programs. She's always helping me with music—listening to different choices at the music store for hours, bringing things home, playing different pieces, asking me what I like. When I find a piece I like and feel like I can skate to, we have to take it to a professional to cut it together.

After the music is cut we start choreographing the program and sketching dress designs. We go to the dressmaker and she shows us fabrics and ideas. Then she makes a mock-up and we go back for fittings. Summer at the rink is always an exciting time, looking at all the girls' new dresses for the upcoming season.

The North American Challenge isn't a *huge* event; with just America and Canada competing, it's like a baby international. But it gives you a good idea of what an international Grand Prix is like. Lake Placid was gorgeous and inspiring, having been the site of the Olympics in 1980, where the U.S. hockey team won against amazing odds. I roomed with Jennifer Kirk at the hotel. We'd met at Nationals before, but now we got to know each other better, hanging out as a team, setting up a disco in the hotel's breakfast buffet area, having as much fun as we could.

During the actual competition I kept thinking about how it was my first event competing as a member of the United States team. So when I popped my triple-Sal combination in my short program, I had a stern talk with myself. Popping—a failure to even attempt a jump—was unacceptable. So I really concentrated going into my long program and went for every element. And it worked—I won the competition! It was an amazing feeling to win. I was so proud of myself, of being able to really focus and do what I was capable of. And to celebrate, I spent the night running around having fun with our small U.S. team.

Moving up to the junior level meant I had to really work on getting the rest of my triple jumps—loop, flip, and Lutz. Back home I was working on them, and that summer I started landing the loop once in a while. It took me a while to get the flip, and the Lutz didn't come to me until later in the year.

The next season, 1998–99, was the most exciting one yet. At Junior Regionals I won the gold medal, and then went to Arizona for Sectionals. By that time I could land my triple flip—fairly consistently. Finally, I was able to do a jump ahead of the other skaters at my level! But I made a mistake, one that should have been easily avoidable, in my short program.

Everyone had expected me to win this event, and I was upset with myself in second place after the short program. But I knew I would skate a good long. I'm not sure how, but I managed to just completely relax. I had "... Baby One More Time" by Britney Spears stuck in my head, and I walked around singing it to myself. Right before my warm-up I had a brownie in the competitor's lounge, which put me on a little sugar high.

✳ *My long program at Nationals*

My mom was confused. She kept saying, "I don't think it's smart to be singing. You need to concentrate!" But for whatever reason, it was really helping me. I went out to the ice, and that long was one of my best programs ever. I just trusted my body, letting it do what it knew best. I won the gold medal again, and afterward my mom said, "Okay, I guess you can sing Britney Spears."

The high of winning Sectionals was only matched by going to Nationals in Salt Lake City. It was February 1999, and the city had already begun building the arenas for the 2002 Olympics. My long program would be held in the same arena where the Olympic skating would take place. At the practice session I took a good look at everything, just completely amazed, thinking, *Wow, this is where the Olympics is going to be, on* this ice. And as much as I was concentrating on the Nationals, I couldn't help but wonder if I'd be back there in three years.

I made two small errors in my long program, stepping out of and two-footing a jump. I placed second to Sara Wheat, and Jennifer Kirk came in third. Once again I was disappointed not to have skated my best. I had to admit my expectations had been greater, after winning both Regionals and Sectionals.

But as always the rest of the week was fun. It's always a big process for me, shopping for party clothes a few weeks before Nationals, and I had a really cute dress that year. I watched Naomi compete in her first senior event against

Michelle Kwan, and she gave the performance of her life. There was a lot of excitement that night.

That season ended on a really high note. Sara Wheat and I were sent to the Val Gardena Winter Trophy competition. It was my first real international event, and the town where it was held, Ortisei in northern Italy, was unbelievably picturesque. It's in the Alps, an ancient and almost magical little town on the side of a mountain. The kind of town where there aren't any skate shops—unlucky

✳ *Junior Nationals, 1999—me, Sara Wheat, Jennifer Kirk, and Elizabeth Kwon*

✳ *Very excited to win the silver medal!*

for me, since I had forgotten my guards. For the whole week I had to walk carefully in my skates on the mats, or tiptoe around so I didn't ruin my blades.

The rink there was semi-enclosed, so during the day the sunlight shone on the ice. If you weren't careful in practice you'd be blinded. And then at night it was very chilly. I sat under a blanket when I wasn't competing, to keep warm and to keep from walking on my blades. I must have looked like one of the spectators, but it worked.

The American team was small, just four of us, and I remember watching Worlds on TV together while we were there. It was a really nice event—even the hotel was amazing. In the morning they would ask us what we wanted for dinner, then cook the most wonderful food for us during the day. By the end of the trip we thought all international events would be that nice, but now I know—it was the nicest competition I've ever been to!

I skated fairly well, winning my second international competition, and they gave me a huge trophy, a gold pin, flowers, the works.

Once the competition was over my mom and I spent some time exploring Austria, Switzerland, and Germany, and stopping to see Saint Moritz, where Mr. Nicks had once won the World Championships.

That summer I continued to train, and I finally landed

my triple Lutz. I also skated with the Champions on Ice tour for the first time. That night I was in awe in the dressing room, looking around at all these Olympic medalists. I was so excited and wanted to explore the backstage area. I decided to go peek out and see what the arena looked like with all the people.

The show was at the Arrowhead Pond, an arena that holds something like 20,000 people, and the place was packed. When I performed, the darkness of the arena, with the ice lit only by spotlights, totally confused me and I skated in the wrong direction through the first part of my program! But the show was really fun, and a really good experience—something that really finished such an incredible season, and looking forward to my first year as a senior competitor.

Chapter Five

SENIOR COMPETITOR
1999 TO 2000

UP TO THAT POINT, EVERYTHING HAD HAPPENED gradually for me, a steady process. You make it to the next level, seeing what it takes, trying new things, driving everywhere, rescheduling school, going to bed early. It all felt really natural. I always keep what I'm doing organized in my mind. I never stay up late unless there's a specific party or celebration—I always have a plan. It's a matter of listening to what my body needs and just following that instinct. I don't feel deprived. I work hard and stay disciplined, but it's always for a purpose. I need to feel a sense of accomplishment.

My mom says I'm very competitive in general, though it's hard for me to see exactly how. I've definitely always had a desire to be the best. That has pushed me. And I've always worked very hard on the ice. I'm kind of a perfectionist, but even in school I almost always got A's; and if I didn't, I'd go back and ask why not, and what I needed to do to improve my grade. I never had a problem with deadlines or homework. I made sure my work was done, and that I'd done the best I could.

A lot of elite athletes just have this sense of knowing—what you need to do, what you are able to do. You just understand your plan. It's simple: You go in every day and you work, you're motivated, you want to win Regionals, it's your dream to go to Nationals, and so on.

I guess it comes down to the fact that I'm very motivated to keep improving. I could really see a lot of improvement in my skating as I moved up through each level, and at the same time I was skating with much more advanced girls, like Naomi, which kept me on my toes. It's so great to be able to train with someone who's better, because it pushes you.

And then the hard work pays off in these miraculous ways, like being on TV for the first time that September, in my first Keri Lotion Pro Am. And, even more amazing, being sent to my first Junior Grand Prix in November 1999, in Sweden.

There are six Grand Prix events for senior skaters each year. You get sent to two events, or three if you're placed in the top six skaters in the world, and the top skaters in these events qualify for the Grand Prix final. Unfortunately I had to miss my first Junior Grand Prix because of a growth plate injury in my heel. Missing it was extremely disappointing, since it meant I wouldn't be able to qualify for the Junior Grand Prix final that year. But I took a rest, healed, and made it to my second event: the Salchow Trophy, in Stockholm.

We had a big U.S.A. team that year, and I remember the team dinner, with all the skaters at one table, our parents at another, and the coaches at a third. We took up the whole place. The entrée choice was between moose or salmon—we were in Sweden, after all! I'm an adventurous eater, so I ordered the moose steak. The meat came out and it was completely rare. It was raw in the middle, and the other skaters tried to help by putting the steak over the candles on the table to cook it more. It wasn't successful, but it was entertaining!

My short program went well, and I placed first. My long was only okay, placing me third, but with my short scores I won the overall competition. There are mixed feelings at an event like that: I'm always upset when I don't skate well, but of course I'm also happy to win. As much as you're there to compete against other skaters, I feel like I'm really competing with myself, constantly trying to improve. So even when I win, I think a lot more about how well I skated, and what I need to do to improve the next time.

As a winner I found out that at the Salchow Trophy they don't actually give you the trophy. They have a case in which they keep all the real trophies, and the winners take home a photograph of theirs. Those of us who had won were kind of disappointed and were definitely surprised. But we also got a beautiful medal and gifts (pearl necklaces for the girls!), so there really wasn't any reason to complain.

And winning qualified me to perform in the exhibition skate, something I love to do. You're so much more relaxed, and your program can be really artistic. It's a nice way to end a competitive event.

Back home I competed in Sectionals—Sweden had conflicted with Regionals, so I was let out of that competition with a "bye," a sort of free pass to the next event. At Sectionals my programs were technically more difficult than the other girls', and I won the gold. The most exciting thing about that was I qualified to go to Cleveland, to compete in my first Nationals as a senior skater. I'd just turned fifteen a few weeks earlier. I couldn't wait—after all this time, I'd be up against my toughest competition yet.

I don't know if I can even describe what an amazing feeling it was to be competing against Michelle and Naomi for the first time. Naomi and I were especially competitive at that point, but more than that, I was just so excited to be at the senior level and competing for a spot on the U.S. World team.

In general, though, there were really no expectations for me. The press, the other skaters—everyone—agreed: "She's someone to watch, a promising skater." I had potential, but no one was expecting me to medal.

In Cleveland, my practice sessions went fairly well. Then my short program was my best ever. I skated in the

✳ *My jaw drops as I'm placed first after the short program at my first Nationals as a senior.*

last group, knowing that Naomi and Michelle had already skated but not knowing their scores or ranks. I was really focused and excited and my program was perfect, entirely clean. At the end I got a standing ovation from the audience. I slowly got off the ice, wanting to stay out there and enjoy the moment forever. I had no idea where I'd be placed as we waited for my scores. When they were announced and my name came up ahead of Michelle's, my jaw just dropped. To be in first place at my first Nationals was a dream come true.

The attention and media that night were unbelievable. Suddenly everyone wanted to talk to me, and the buzz began. That night was the turning point in my relationship with the media. Now I was known; now there were expectations.

So going into my long program I was more nervous than ever. I skated well through the whole program until I made one mistake at the end that cost me. I fell on the last jump, a triple toe. In the end, I placed second overall, taking home the silver medal at my first Senior Nationals—my biggest accomplishment yet. There was definitely a twinge of disappointment at not winning because of that last mistake, but I was too busy being thrilled to have made the world team. And I was also busy doing lots of interviews and magazine photo shoots in the next few weeks.

✳ *Long program at the 2000 Nationals*

✳ *On the podium next to Michelle Kwan at Nationals*

Even though I had qualified to go to the World Championships, the International Skating Union had a rule that skaters who hadn't turned fifteen by July 1 couldn't compete in Senior Worlds. Of course I wouldn't turn fifteen until October, but I still had a loophole: If I placed in the top three at Junior Worlds, I would be "grandfathered in" and allowed to compete in Senior Worlds.

So I set off for Obersdorf, Germany. Before we left I was having a problem with my right calf and not able to train very hard, but I tried to work around it. Everyone was looking at Junior Worlds as a technicality, assuming it would be no big deal. Even I wasn't worried, thinking, *Oh, it'll be fine.*

Junior Worlds is a huge event, even if I had my eye on the bigger World Championships. It was much bigger than the Junior Grand Prix event I'd been to. The U.S. had a big team, and was considered the future in American skating: pairs dancers Tanith Belbin and Ben Agosto, Jennifer Kirk, Matt Savoie. It was an exciting group to be in.

At the qualifying round I performed decently, securing second place. But things fell apart in my short program. I just wasn't prepared. I landed my first combo perfectly, but missed my triple Lutz footwork. I was in shock and couldn't snap out of it. I was so disappointed, and I just wasn't able to get over it and move on. I became tentative and I doubted my abilities. And then I missed my double axel, which I never miss at all, and my ranking went way down.

I was devastated. I couldn't get over the fact that I'd just blown my chance to win Junior Worlds, and possibly my chance to go to Senior Worlds. I was crying and upset, but in the back of my mind I was still thinking I'd be able to pull it out in the long program, have a good skate, and get third overall. Mr. Nicks had a talk with me, and we started thinking about the long program.

And I did improve, dramatically—my long program

was nearly clean, even better than my Nationals debut. Unfortunately I skated in the second-to-last group, and at that round the judges were holding marks for the next group. I thought my work was done. I happily changed and sat with the U.S. team to watch the last group. With each strong performance and skater placing ahead of me, my heart sank, and two skaters later I realized I wouldn't be moving up. I'd given it my best shot, but it wasn't good enough. I finished in sixth place. I wouldn't be going to Worlds.

After that I just wanted to get home. As always the final party was fun, but after a letdown like that, it was hard for me to be around people and handle the disappointment. You need time to yourself, to process the whole thing and reflect.

Like all disappointing events, only time can help. I didn't watch the Worlds on TV that year, just got back to training, moving on to the next thing and looking forward to the next season when, surely, everything would finally fall into place.

Chapter Six

A SETBACK
2000 TO 2001

THE ATTENTION I STARTED GETTING AT NATIONALS kept up through the summer of 2000. I was invited to the Teen Choice Awards and was interviewed by several magazines, including *People*.

I trained at home and at Lake Arrowhead, and a little in Sun Valley.

Natasha, as usual, was having a typical summer, hanging out with her friends. We went shopping together and saw movies. And she continued to practice the piano. We were lucky with our favorite pastimes. I'd tried piano when I was younger but didn't love it, and she'd tried ice skating but didn't like the cold. We can appreciate and support each other's interests without directly competing, which makes it much easier to get along.

Something weird happened that August. I was mostly

training at home, but had gone up to Lake Arrowhead to do one of their Hot Summer Nights shows. Stretching on the floor, I felt a crack in my back. At first it felt really good. But then I got up, and I couldn't step on my right foot at all. The pain was intense, and I didn't understand what had happened.

For a week I couldn't bend forward or backward. So I took it easy, waiting to see, and slowly the pain went away. I was still aware of it, but it wasn't bothering me enough to take time off.

By the time the season started I'd forgotten all about my back. Mr. Nicks and I discussed the possibility of sending me to Junior Grand Prix events, instead of Seniors, because I was still young and he thought it might be good experience. But I really wanted to compete at the next level.

So I went to my first Senior Grand Prix, the Nations Cup in Germany.

Germany is not my favorite spot. I skated terribly again, just as I had in Obersdorf. I missed the triple Lutz combo in the short, but a lot of girls made mistakes, and I ended up placing fourth. I hadn't missed a jump in practice all week, but I couldn't get over that mistake. I kept running it through my head, over and over, seeing myself falling, worrying that it would happen again. Instead of making me more prepared, my obsession created doubt and a problem where there had been none. I fell on the Lutz in my long program, too, and then on the next jump, and then again on my last one. Falling three times was incredibly upsetting. How could I let that happen?

But I had to find a way to get over it quickly—the Cup of Russia Grand Prix was taking place in Saint Petersburg the very next week. I went back to practicing and tried to find positive thoughts.

This was my first trip to Russia. I was so excited to see the country my mom had grown up in, and the people there were so welcoming. The audience there was especially supportive because they knew my mother was Russian.

Of course, it was also insanely freezing there. And the meals were a little difficult—they really revolved more around drinking than eating. There were so many glasses and bottles of vodka at dinner, you couldn't see the table!

The arena for the event was the biggest I'd ever seen. It looked like a gigantic enclosed football field; the rink only took up one quarter of the space. It was an interesting place to compete. Both of my programs were clean, earning me standing ovations. It was such a huge accomplishment for me. The competition was tough, and I ended up fourth, but I was so happy with my performances and so happy to skate well after the disastrous event in Germany.

✳ *Freezing with my mom and sister on my first trip to Russia*

The next day I was invited to be part of the exhibition, which didn't go quite as smoothly as the competition had. I remember pulling the tape of my music out of my skate bag, and handing it over without listening or practicing to it. Out on the ice, everything was fine until I ended my program, but for some reason the music was still going. Way too late, I realized I'd handed over an uncut version of my music. So instead of four minutes, the piece was running much longer—more than five minutes total. An extra minute doesn't sound like much, but in a huge arena, in front of a crowd, making stuff up after you've already skated an entire program is, to say the least, *exhausting*. I faked my way through the end of the song and then just collapsed! Definitely not a mistake I'd be making twice.

After the exhibition I was presented with a special award. A lot of people had thought my fourth-place standing was unfair—I guess a lot of people who saw the competition thought I should have been placed higher. To recognize my performance, a newspaper in Saint Petersburg, the *Labor*, gave me a gorgeous hand-painted Russian box inscribed with my award—being the "most beautiful skater" at the event. The gift, and the local support it represented, meant so much to me.

Back home that December, I was training for a Pro Am (professional-amateurs' competition—these are really just amateur events now). I noticed that my landings were kind of painful, more and more so with each jump. My back was acting up again, even though it had been months since that ominous popping sound during my stretching.

Mr. Nicks and I conferred again, wondering if I should compete. My argument was basically, "It's probably nothing, the Pro Am is in two days. I should just do it." So I went, and I skated really well, but I was in quite a bit of pain.

After that, the pain just kept getting worse and worse. We went to different doctors, skated a little, had X-rays done, tried to train, took a break, then tried training again. It was all pretty unorganized and very frustrating. Everyone had a different opinion, but no one had the answer, and the 2001 Nationals were coming up in a few weeks.

Once again I argued for going. All my hard work was leading to this. I really wanted to compete, and wanted even more to place in the top three so I could finally attend a Senior Worlds. The Olympics were only a year away, and to miss this year's biggest events seemed career-ending. Certainly I needed to go to Worlds before judges would consider me at the Olympics!

"All right, we'll go," Mr. Nicks said to me. "I don't think you're ready, but if you want to compete, I'll support you."

We flew to Boston, and after just one practice, only a couple of jumps into it, I had to stop because the pain had become so intense. I was scared, and I knew I was making the pain a lot worse by continuing to skate. Plus, I wasn't even ready. All the back-and-forth to doctors and taking time off and broken practice sessions hadn't let me prepare properly. It was a terrible decision to have to make, but Mr. Nicks and I held a press conference. I had to withdraw from Nationals. I needed to take the time to heal.

The one bright spot, coming home from Boston, was that just a few weeks later we all moved to a new rink. The Ice Capades Chalet closed down, and we transferred to the brand-new Aliso Viejo Ice Palace. Not only was the rink nicer and newer, Aliso Viejo was only seven minutes from my house. I was now saving tons of time with a shorter commute and, even better, I was driving myself— I'd just gotten my license, after taking driver's ed with my good friend, Christie Baca.

But it was time to get more serious about the problems with my back. I started physical therapy three times a week with Randy Bauer, strengthening my core muscles. I realized that my core wasn't stabilizing my body when I skated. The core exercises began to improve things immediately, and I slowly worked back into my routine, skating three times a week, taking on a few single jumps every other day, moving forward really carefully.

Naomi also had missed that year's Nationals because of

an injury. She had hip problems that never healed. She'd be resting for a while, then come back and skate really strong, then be injured again, on and off. Watching her struggle with this taught me so much. She was never able to overcome her injury, and I learned to be extra cautious whenever anything goes wrong. Now my approach to an injury is: Fix it now. Just take care of it, don't push into anything before you're ready, because the most important thing is your body—you have to take special care of it.

Dr. Westin, a family friend, finally helped us diagnose what was wrong with me. Other doctors had speculated there was a stress fracture, but I had a full-body scan done and no fracture was ever found. At last we found out that I had extreme arthritis in my lower right back joint. The physical therapy was perfect treatment. Even now, if I go a week without doing my core work my back will start hurting again. It's a lot of maintenance, but it's essential.

By the end of March 2001 I was able to practice jumping again. I started focusing on my stroking to improve my speed and edges. I used to have no control over my edges at all, and I'm still learning. It was great to have time to concentrate on this aspect of my skating.

I also had to come up with a new, jump-free routine for the Champions on Ice tour, as well as for Viktor Petrenko's charity event, "Viktory for Kids," which raises money for the Children of Chernobyl Relief Fund.

With no jumps, I thought I needed something else exciting, like a prop. After brainstorming, I decided to try a ribbon program. I wanted to do something interesting, and this was the perfect thing to keep me occupied learning a new skill and distracted from thoughts of jumping. My mom and I spent a lot of time buying ribbons, having them died to match my dress, and learning how to roll them up so they wouldn't get wrinkled. I ruined so many ribbons, skating over and spinning on top of them. And every day I had to iron and starch them because if they're not perfectly straight and structured, they won't fly well.

I loved my new routine, loved trying something new and artistic and challenging. In my first performance, though, at the Viktory for Kids show, things got a little out of hand. I got tangled. And I couldn't get untangled—I was struggling for the longest thirty seconds ever. Someone in the audience laughed, and I was completely mortified! When I finally straightened everything out, the program was great. It was the first, but more importantly the *last*, time I got tangled.

And so, with a lot of hard work and patience, I got through the back injury. Of course I was worried and disappointed, but I tried to focus on something else rather than dwell on my withdrawal from Nationals and missed opportunity to go to Worlds. I kept up with my training while still allowing my body to heal. I improved what I could and accepted what I couldn't do for a while. I kept looking forward, and there was a lot to look forward to. The Olympics were coming up, and after all these years I was a senior competitor and ready to go.

Chapter Seven

ROAD TO THE OLYMPICS
2001 TO 2002

AS I GOT BACK INTO SHAPE THAT SUMMER, WE started working on my new long program. I had skated to music from the opera *Carmen*, by Bizet, years before, and I wanted to again. Mr. Nicks was really against the idea. A lot of skaters have used that music. It's very dramatic, and there are wonderful pieces to choose from. He felt that it was too familiar, and too many other women had used it in competitions before, and he especially remembered "the Battle of the Carmens," at the 1988 Olympics, when Katarina Witt and Debi Thomas both skated their long programs to it. After several of my unsuccessful attempts to convince him that I loved the music and it was perfect for me, he heard it on the radio one day, and suddenly changed his mind. He thought, *This* is *perfect for Sasha.*

So I got to work on the choreography and costume. I

met with a Spanish ballerina named Sophia, who helped me bring out the character of Carmen in my skating. Since I hadn't competed much the year before, we decided to keep the same short program, which let me devote more time to my new free program that I was thrilled with.

I also had a little more time to deal with the problems we were having with the Carmen costume. One designer made a dress that completely didn't stretch—and I knew well by then what a disaster that could be. We couldn't seem to find anything that worked, and then we just ran out of time. For competitions I was wearing one of Jenni Meno's dresses or one of my own practice outfits.

As my back was healing that spring, I'd worked with a coach in Washington D.C. on relearning my triple jumps. Trying to land them, after almost four months of not jumping, was scary, so Nick would skate with me using a harness. The harness worked kind of like a fishing pole, with Nick holding it and me on the other end. It allowed me to land with less force, easing me back into all of my jumps, helping me gain back my confidence.

Later that summer we used the harness to work on trying to land a quad Salchow. No woman skater had ever landed this jump in competition, and it's very difficult to even practice. I'd tried it with Mr. Nicks a few times the summer before, but I was just killing myself with the landings—or, rather, falls—so we invested in a harness of our own and found Matt Smith, a coach from Canada who would hold me while I tried the jump.

I worked on the quad about three times a week. I was always on the ice right before the hockey players' practice. At exactly 12:30 an incredibly loud buzzer would go off, and about twenty of these huge guys would come storming onto the ice, completely oblivious to me. I'd try to fight them for a little room, just one more jump, but of course they usually won.

I landed the quad on two feet that summer, but wouldn't officially land it until a few months later.

In the meantime I had been invited to the Goodwill Games, which were being held in Australia, after Sarah Hughes backed out. The Goodwill Games were started in 1986 in Moscow, Russia, as a way to ease tensions during the Cold War. The 1980 Olympics in Moscow were boycotted by the United States, and Ted Turner wanted to start an event that would be held regardless of politics. Now that the Cold War is over, the Games raise money for youth charities.

I was thrilled to be included, especially after missing Nationals and Worlds that year. It was incredibly reassuring to know that the skating community hadn't forgotten about me during my hiatus. And the trip was a blast—

my mom cashed in all of her frequent-flier miles to get us first-class tickets. It was the best flight ever. We got terrific meals and private movies and great seats. I didn't want to get off the plane!

Brisbane was a big city with a lot to see. My friend Johnny Weir was there with his mom, and the four of us toured around together. Most of my time was taken up with practice, though, especially since the rink was an hour away from where we were staying. At the competition I double-footed a few jumps and placed fourth, but overall I was ecstatic to be back in competition again.

The day after we got home from Australia was September 11th. I was still jet-lagged and sleeping in, and I remember my mom came to wake me up to watch the news. Like everyone else, we couldn't believe what was happening. We'd flown home at just the right time, since all the airports were now closed. Michelle Kwan had actually gotten stuck in Australia, having stayed there an extra few days. All of my upcoming events, especially the international ones, were now in doubt.

But like everyone we had to get back to the routine. It was my senior year, and I'd decided I really wanted to go back to normal high school, with all the kids I knew from elementary school and junior high. We talked to the school board about my schedule, and I enrolled in Aliso

Niguel High School for partial days. This meant getting up really early, but not for practice—classes started at 7:15. I remember on my first day I got up extra early to do my hair and makeup perfectly, and make sure I had a cute outfit on. I was ready to make my high school debut. It was exhausting!

I loved seeing all my friends again, but the course schedule was as tough as ever to fit in with my skating. I took only a few classes but had to drop one almost immediately. I do remember, though, I had the most amazing economics teacher, Mr. Cheyenne, and of course there were the homecoming and prom dances to look forward to.

In October I had the Finlandia Trophy competition, in Helsinki, Finland. Everyone was still afraid to fly, and it was the first post–9/11 competition the U.S. was sending a team to. My mom was more worried than I was; I assumed it would be safe, especially because the security was so intense.

Helsinki was very cold, dark, and rainy—not my favorite place—but they did have the best breakfast: eggs a million ways, fruit, croissants, the list goes on. At the competition I made a good quad attempt, but fell on the landing. More importantly, I was able to recover from my mistake and still skate a clean program afterward. And I won, my first time to do so at a senior international event. There weren't that many people there, and competition wasn't very strong, but of course I was really happy to win.

A few weeks later, right around my seventeenth birthday, was my first Skate America competition, which was held that year in Colorado Springs. Mr. Nicks and I decided to put the quad in the program again.

And that's when I finally landed it—in practice at Skate America. ABC was filming and caught it, and whenever I watch the tape I can remember how great it felt, how just completely amazing it was.

During the event my short program was pretty good, though they marked me pretty low. So, even more than usual, I was very, very nervous for my long program. Colorado Springs is very high up, and generally at that altitude it's hard to make it through a four-minute program. I was worried about this, and even more so about the quad. Before I went onto the ice I hugged Mr. Nicks and cried, "I don't wanna go out there!"

"It'll be all right," he said, pushing me, nicely, toward the rink. "You'll be fine."

I still couldn't calm my nerves. I got on the ice, trying to brace myself. I missed the takeoff on my quad and did a single instead. And unfortunately I wasn't able to realize, *That's okay, you still have the rest of the program to do well.* I just kept making mistakes through the whole program, losing more and more confidence. At one point I thought, *Just get me off the ice!* It was terrible, and embarrassing. And it was probably the worst performance of my life. Strangely, I landed my last two jumps—at that altitude, I thought I'd have been too tired by the end, but that's the kind of weird day it was. I was so crushed, we skipped the day-after banquet. My mom took me to Denver for some birthday shopping, but I just wanted to get home. Not my best birthday.

At home I had other things to think about. Homecoming was coming up, and I went with a group of friends. It was my first dance, and I couldn't believe how insanely crowded it was. They held it at the school, and I kept getting squished between people—it was hard to find room to dance!

You're only as good as your last performance, so as soon as I could, I shook off the Skate America event and looked forward to the Trophée Lalique, in Bercy, in Paris, France. And finally I had a new dress for my program! I'd worn makeshift dresses to the Goodwill Games and Skate America, and at last I could wear the real one.

My new dress was a beautiful red outfit, with black fishnet sleeves and rhinestones all over it. Unfortunately I soon discovered another costume pitfall: The fishnet kept getting caught on the rhinestones when I moved my arms. In France I actually missed my Lutz because my arm got stuck. At the hotel that night my mom cut off as many rhinestones as she could, but I still had to be really careful.

They scheduled the Ladies' performances far into the night, after the audience got a dinner break. We were all kind of upset, not feeling like we could perform our best when we were half asleep. I placed third, not my best skate, but it was my first medal at a Grand Prix event and therefore was pretty exciting.

Around Christmas I convinced my parents that one more kitten, in addition to Meow and Natasha's dog, Mocha, wouldn't make that big of a difference in the house. They finally relented, and we brought home Mia, a tiny puff of white fur.

I snuck Mia along with me to the 2002 Nationals, which were also that year's Olympic Trials. They were being held in Los Angeles that year, an easy drive from our house. It was a great situation—beautiful hotel, familiar area, no jetlag, huge arena, and all my family and friends there to cheer me on.

After all the costume problems I'd been having, we still hadn't found a perfect dress. The day of the long, I decided I'd just wear one of my black practice dresses. We found a red crystal rose, which we secured to the back of the dress, and a red flower for my hair. It was simple and perfect and, best of all, comfortable to skate in.

✳ *With my silver medal at the 2000 Nationals. Off to the Olympics!*

There were a lot of really strong U.S. skaters that year, so I was incredibly nervous and anxious about making the Olympic team. Plus, it had been two years since I'd skated at Nationals. The pressure was almost overwhelming. Mr. Nicks and I had talked about the quad and pulled it from my program, deciding it was just too much on top of everything else.

Everyone came to see me skate at Nationals. My dad, who is usually very laid back about my skating, competitions included, was there, and so was Natasha, and a lot of other family and friends. It helped having their support, but it also made me that much more anxious that I perform well.

Once again I was skating in the final group in the short program, and I had no idea how anyone else had done. As was becoming more and more my routine, I took myself through everything one step at a time. I talked myself through it by just making one little request of myself at a time: *You only have to put on your dress. All you have to do is warm up. You just have to stretch.* And then I was on the ice, and everything felt great. My short was clean, and I was so excited to place second in this incredible group of women.

But there was still the pressure of the long program. At that point, everything is so final—like you're walking to the ends of the earth, thinking the whole time, *This is IT*. All of us were terribly nervous.

Again, I made myself go through everything step by step. Michelle was really nervous, too, and we were so caught up in our own routines, we bumped into each other on the ice during the warm-up. I got off the ice after the warm-up, and went back behind a curtain, took off my skates, and lay down on the floor to try to calm myself. My heart was beating so hard, it was shaking my whole body.

The waiting is the worst part for everyone. But once I got out there and could feel ice under my feet, it all came back. I knew what to do.

I skated one of my best performances ever that night. I landed six triples, and put my hand down on an improvised seventh. I skated enthusiastically into my spins and spirals and throughout the program. *Carmen* inspired me, and I skated passionately. It earned me second place, with Michelle in first and Sarah in third. I couldn't stop smiling, couldn't stop thinking, *Oh my God, I made the Olympic team!*

And then, nonstop action. Ceremonies, drug testing, paperwork, receptions, get your stuff, competitors' party, four hours of sleep because everyone's celebrating in the room next door, exhibition practice, team meetings, exhibition. That night after making the team, we all went to an

Olympic party. While I was there, Peggy Fleming handed me a little blue Tiffany box. The card was congratulating me, wishing me luck, and signed by Peggy. The gift was a silver picture frame. I couldn't believe it—like everything else that was happening, it was just magical.

And then, back to training. I had about a month before I needed to be in Salt Lake City. When I got back to school my economics teacher had put balloons around my chair. He also brought in a video of my short program from the Nationals to show to the whole class. I was so embarrassed! At least it was a good performance—and of course I was flattered, too.

I kept busy, avoiding the crowded ice in Aliso Viejo by going up to Lake Arrowhead for a while. Mr. Nicks met me there later, and we worked on getting me ready for the most important event of my life.

Chapter Eight

THE OLYMPIC DREAM
TRAINING AND OPENING CEREMONIES

AFTER THAT, EVERYTHING STARTED MOVING REALLY fast. A few days after Nationals I was due to run with the Olympic torch in San Diego, near where my grandparents live. I'd been asked several weeks before, and all through Nationals there was a little worry in the back of my head: *What if I don't make the team?* It wouldn't have felt right to carry the Olympic symbol without actually being on the U.S. team—but now I was, and I felt incredibly honored and excited.

I wore the official white track suit and white gloves with silver Olympic rings on them. My parents and sister and grandparents all came to watch me. It was dark outside, and you could see all the lights of the boardwalk glittering in the water, and of course the torch itself, burning brightly.

✳ *Lighting the Olympic torch*

My run wasn't very long, just a short stretch down
the boardwalk, but the torch was much heavier than I'd
expected. Just a few steps and my arm was burning! But
I was just thinking about the Olympics, about what an
amazing tradition it is, and how I was now a part of it.

On the plane to Salt Lake City a few weeks later, I

✳ Me as a baby

✳ Me and Mom
on the beach

✳ My love for ice cream
started very early.

Skating in Pasadena. My mom made the dress I'm wearing.

Me and Natasha on the beach in L.A.

* Practicing

* The view from my
  bedroom at the
  Laguna Niguel house

✳ Mom, me, and Natasha
in the hot springs in
Sun Valley

✳ 2000 U.S. Nationals—
short program. Dick
Button called this "the
Sasha curl."

* Me, Daddy, and Natasha

* Me and Natasha with Meow Meow and Mocha. Meow Meow didn't really enjoy this Christmas card photo shoot.

* Natasha cheering me on

* Mia at the Olympics. I let her borrow my official jacket even though she wasn't competing.

✳ 2002 Olympics
practice

✳ At practice

✳ *2002 Skate Canada—*
short program

2003 U.S. Nationals—
short program

*2003 Skate Canada—
long program*

✳ 2004 Champions on Ice—
as Eliza Doolittle in
My Fair Lady *before…*

✳ *…and after*

✳ 2004 Worlds
medals ceremony

✳ 2005 U.S. Nationals—
short program

✳ The 2005 U.S.
Nationals medalists

*✳ 2005 U.S. Nationals—
long program*

stared down at the mountains, just thinking, *Oh my God, it's finally here. The next time I'm looking down on these mountains, I'll have been to the Olympics!* Everything felt that way—this is the last time I'll do this, whatever "this" was, before the Olympics. You're constantly aware of what a monumental turning point it is. Everything I'd worked for had led up to this moment.

The airport was covered with Olympic decorations, memorabilia, souvenirs. I'd done an ad for Visa a year earlier, and they used the silhouette of my picture for a huge poster that was plastered everywhere. Of course no one could tell it was me, and I had to insist that I recognized the outfit I'd been wearing. Even if you couldn't see my face, seeing myself as a part of the Olympic advertising was an amazing feeling. I was really there.

From the airport the athletes were taken straight to a huge warehouse near the University of Utah. The first stop was accreditation for the U.S. team. We went around with shopping carts to all these different tables and booths, gathering at least three huge suitcases' worth of clothing and supplies, all with the Olympic rings on it. Then we went to the information session, where they told us how the Olympic Village, set up on the university campus, worked, and what we'd need to know for the next two weeks. We each got a cell phone that only worked during the Games, were sized for our Olympic team rings, received instructions on where the dining rooms were—one inside, one under a tent covering the football field. And from there we were bussed into the Village, to the U.S.A. house. It really was like a village—there was even a spa, a place to get a facial or manicure, and a mini movie theater.

I shared the tiniest dorm imaginable with three other girls. Naomi Lang, one of the U.S. team ice dancers, and I were in one half of the room, with a wall between us and the room of Sarah Hughes and Kyoko Ina. You can imagine four girls with all their stuff—plus all the stuff we'd just been given—sharing this ridiculously small space and one bathroom. It was a mess! The only reason we had room for our clothes was that the beds were set high up, so we could stuff everything under them.

It would have been an awesome experience to stay in the Village for fun, but for training, with all the nervousness of being at the Olympics, it was quite a challenge. I decided to stay just for a few days, then fly back home for the two weeks to train before the competition. While I was there I went to one practice in the main arena. It was crowded with gigantic Olympic rings, on the ice, on the boards, on the flags hanging from the rafters. But otherwise the arena was a ghost town, no media or spectators—no skaters, even, just me and Michelle.

The opening ceremonies were held the day after we arrived. For the athletes, it was a really long process. In groups of athletes from each country, we marched something like three miles to the stadium where the ceremonies were held, and of course it was freezing. I kept complaining about the walk—it was a long trip, and a lot of it was uphill—and some of the other athletes were laughing, like, "You're an athlete! It's just walking!" It was hard to explain, "No, I skate, and that's *it*." Back then, I wasn't used to walking. And I've never gotten used to being so cold!

But at least I managed to stay pretty warm. I wore long underwear, fleece pants, a couple of thermals, two turtlenecks, a sweater, a scarf, two pairs of gloves, two pairs of socks. We'd been given official black boots, but they were only made of vinyl, so my mom and I found some really warm sheepskin boots. They were beige, so we had them covered with black tape to match the rest of the team. My feet were warm and so much more comfortable than they would have been!

I met a lot of people on the walk over. I'm not a shy person—I was just walking up and down our group, the whole American team, asking people, "Hey, what do you do?" I met a bunch of skiers and speed skaters.

We also stopped at the college gymnasium on the way for a special meeting with President Bush. He congratulated us and shook our hands. Yet again I was struck by how huge this whole experience was, how amazing it was to be part of it.

The U.S. team was the last to enter the ceremony. It was still light out when we arrived at the holding area, and we had to wait until dark—hours later—to enter the stadium. Again, I was grateful for my warm outfit, topped off by my official Olympics beret. And the slow procession was worth it when we finally went inside the stadium. That was one of the most incredible moments in the

✳ *Coming into the arena for the opening ceremonies. Completely lit up—amazing!*

entire Olympic experience for me—turning the corner and walking inside. It was breathtaking. The huge outdoor arena was all lit up, and the audience had been given signs and lights to hold, creating a beautiful, colorful pattern. On the floor of the stadium a curvy walkway wound around a pond-shaped ice rink, and as we walked, everyone exploded with applause and cheers for our team.

At last, we were seated. It was so exciting, listening to the music and introductions. Kristi Yamaguchi skated, and the Olympic hockey team from 1980 lit the torch at the top of the stadium, where it would burn for the rest of the Winter Games.

A few minutes after we were seated, a Secret Service agent came by. President Bush had arrived, and they had to figure out where he should sit. They decided to put him six rows behind me, to my left, and I was so excited, I called my mom to tell her.

Then, ten minutes later, the Secret Service man came back and said, "He's supposed to be in row fifty-six, seat number thirty-five." Row fifty-six was *my* row. I was sitting next to team leader Kristy Krawl and skater Tim Goebel, and I was in seat thirty-five. "Okay," the Secret Service guy said, "you guys scoot over, and put this blanket down on the seat."

So this whole time I'm thrilled and elated just to be at

the Olympics, and now this! I called my mom back and said, "Guess what? The president's going to be sitting *next* to me!"

"Oh, sure," she said, with lots of doubt. "I think you must have misunderstood. That can't be possible."

So as soon as I could, I called her back again and handed the phone to President Bush. "Could you say hello to my mom?" I asked. He was really nice about it, took the phone, and talked to her for three or four minutes. My mom said she almost fell off her chair!

Then he talked to me a little bit. The performance was now a group of skaters carrying long poles attached to silk animals, kind of like kites. I remember him saying, "I like the horse the best," and asking me which one was my favorite. He also wished me luck. When I asked if he was going to stick around to watch some of the events in the next two weeks, he replied, "No, I have to go fight a war."

After that, everyone started handing the president their cell phones until he had to get up to make a short speech and then leave.

I couldn't believe it. I'd made it all the way to the Olympics, and already my life had changed in ways I'd never even imagined!

Elated, I went back home and started training in Lake Arrowhead, mainly because its altitude is higher than Salt

Lake City's. Practicing there would help build up my endurance, making it easier to skate in the high altitude of Salt Lake. Plus, I had less than two weeks before my events, too much time to hang around the Village. And I needed time to be away from all the buzz and take a break from skating in the intense media spotlight of the Olympics, and make sure everything was 100 percent ready to go. I stayed with Allison for a while, and for the rest of the time my mom and I got a room at the Lake Arrowhead Resort so I could focus.

And then it was really time to go.

Chapter Nine

DREAM BECOMES REALITY
THE 2002 WINTER GAMES

BACK IN SALT LAKE CITY MY MOM AND I CHECKED into a hotel, sneaking in my kitten, Mia. My dad and Natasha had flown out with her so they could all be there to support me in the audience at my events. A bunch of my family and friends and even our interior decorators were there, too.

Before I left, my skating club had thrown me a good-luck party, and I brought a bunch of their gifts with me to set up in my room. I put lots of candles around the room and kept the little memory book Tiffany had made for me out on the table. I made myself feel really at home. Just being at the Olympics is so stressful, you have to do whatever you can to calm yourself down—like bring your kitten so she can sleep with you at night.

I had three days before my short program, and my

Practice session—me, Michelle Kwan, Sarah Hughes, and Sarah's coach, Robin Wagner. Can you tell we're all nervous?

practices were all going well. I was very focused all the time, but I did take a night off to have dinner with our family friends the Westins. One of their daughters used to skate with me in the summer, but they lived in Salt Lake City. So they knew the most amazing restaurant out in the countryside, on an old estate. It was a wonderful experience to relax and have fun, and get away from the center of activity, in the midst of all the stress. The

Westins had told the restaurant manager that I was skating in the Olympics, so when my dessert arrived it had been decorated with these little fireworks. The whole night was really special and made me feel very supported.

The women's part of the figure skating competition takes place over three days—short programs the first day, a day off, and then the day of the long programs. I skated first in my warm-up group in the short. I was wearing a new dress, made by Mare Talbot, who has made many dresses for me since I was eleven. I'd spent a lot of time with her picking out crystals and sequins, all in different shades of blue. It really sparkled.

The night of my short program I went through my usual preparations and warm-up. Then I finished tying my boots, adjusted my dress, and waited for my name to be called.

As usual I tried to take each element at a time, not dwelling too far ahead or behind on what I was doing right then. After so much practice, skating is so much about muscle memory, what your body has done eighty million times and knows so well. Your brain isn't working so much as it's just saying, *Push, smile, faster.* One word at a time, to keep you going.

I landed my first jump. Then my flip was clean, and after that I was just completely happy. I (almost) forgot about being nervous. I flew into my death-drop spin, pushed really fast into my spirals, thinking constantly about speed and extension. My last jump was the easiest of all of them, and I was, like, *Okay, keep it together for this last jump*. But I'd already started the double axel, landed it, and at that point I was just overwhelmed with complete, total relief. When you finish your last jump in a competition like that, you're so happy, it's like a party going inside you.

I concentrated on flying like the wind in my footwork, reminding myself to be sharp and quick, trying not to let my tired legs slow down. Then one last combination spin, and the music ended. I finished the program to a roar of applause—an American had finished a clean program! I didn't want to get off the ice. It was exactly what I'd wanted, exactly what I'd dreamed of.

I took my time getting off the ice and went to the kiss-and-cry area, where I gave Mr. Nicks a huge hug. I knew from the look on his face that he was *so* proud of me. I couldn't stop smiling as I waited for my scores, and then smiled even more when the judges gave me really good marks.

My mind was already jumping to the long program, to what I needed to do in practice the next day, how to make it perfect. But Mr. Nicks stopped me. "Dear, just relax and enjoy tonight," he said. "I don't want you even thinking about the long. You were great. We'll talk about it tomorrow."

After doing some interviews in "the mixed zone"—a room set off for the media and athletes to meet—I went to watch the rest of the skaters on the TV in the warm-up area. At the end of the night, I was in third place. Anything could happen now—I could even medal.

The next morning I woke up and read about myself in the paper, kind of patting myself on the back. Then a little voice in my head piped up: *Great—but it's not over.* It was time to focus on the next day.

The day in between your programs is always more relaxed. You practice a little, then take it easy. You feel like you have all the time in the world. It's the night before when all the tension starts up again. But even then, you're still thinking, *Oh, I still have a practice before the competition tomorrow.*

It was *so* hard to get to sleep that night. I wanted everything to be perfect, and I didn't want to regret anything. I went over my program in my head, again and again. It was almost impossible to stop thinking about it.

And then it was the day of my long program. I went to practice in the morning, went through all my jumps, and everything seemed fine. Then I went to warm up my last jump, the triple Lutz, and it was terrible. At first I just thought, *Whoa, that was really bad.*

But then it got worse. The more I did it, the worse it

was. I wasn't even close—I was doing, like, two and a half turns, landing forward, then smashing down on my side. I kept practicing it even after all the other girls had left. This just couldn't be happening. But it was. Finally I let it go, did a few doubles, and left.

I remembered lying awake in bed the night before, picturing the jump, going through it over and over in my head. I'd thought about it too much. I'd changed the timing that my body naturally knew, and now I couldn't get it back.

I was a mess, but as always Mr. Nicks was really calm. "It's okay," he said, "you'll have it tonight." But I was too distraught to believe him.

Back at the hotel, I dozed a little, but was too preoccupied to rest long. When I woke up, I had a brilliant idea. I turned to my mom and said, "We have to find a video of when I did it right!"

For what seemed like hours, my mom made phone call after phone call from the hotel room, asking anyone and everyone we knew in the area, "Do you have a tape of the Nationals?" Finally our friend Jed Hopkins said yes, and he lived nearby. He dropped it off at the hotel, and we got a conference room to use the VCR.

I watched that tape over and over. After a while I kind of got the timing back in my head, and walked through the takeoff on the floor until it felt right. I'm sure watching it was the only reason I was able to do the triple Lutz that night. But the whole episode had made me extra jittery. Competition day is a series of lasts: In the morning there's still another practice, and then when you're coming back from practice you realize, *There's no more practice. All I have left is a nap, and after that, time to get ready.* After you've done your makeup and left your hotel room it really hits you: *This is the last time I'm leaving the hotel, this is the last time I'm on the elevator.* Everything you do, you're doing for the last time until the competition is over.

I made my way through the insane number of security checkpoints. They went through my bags each time while I stood there, nervous and freezing cold.

At the rink, most of the girls were already done, relaxing and enjoying themselves. Those of us who had just arrived were being chased, as usual, by the media. You almost have to hide from the cameramen. Sometimes they're right in your face, trying to get shots when you're warming up, and it's really tense. They'll run up to you, three different cameramen at once. I did my best to avoid them and went through my usual warm-up routine. I'd never been so nervous.

I had drawn to skate fourth. Sarah would be second, Michelle fifth, and Irina Slutskaya would skate last.

I wasn't wearing my black practice dress anymore. I now had a red dress with a fiery skirt with black diamonds on it. It fit my *Carmen* music and still had a unique flair that fit my personality.

About ten minutes before I was supposed to skate, I went back to change into my costume. I went through my skating bag, pulling out my dress, my skates, my tights . . . wait. Where were my tights? I searched through again. No tights. This couldn't possibly be happening.

I remembered going through the three checkpoints, with the security guards going through my bag each time, taking things out and rearranging everything. Someone must have accidentally taken my tights out and not put them back. And now here I was, and I couldn't skate without them. This was not possible! My heart just plummeted into my stomach as I thought, *Oh my God, I have no tights, I'm not going to be able to compete in the Olympics!*

I called my mom, who was in the arena, and she was flipping out because it wasn't possible to get back to the hotel, get new tights, and get back to me in time—I only had about eight minutes before I needed to be on the ice.

Then Fumie Suguri walked in. She'd just gotten off the ice and was about to change back into her regular clothes. "Fumie!" I said. "Can I *please* borrow your tights?"

"Sure," she told me, and right there she took off the

tights she was wearing and handed them to me. I couldn't believe it—I only had a couple minutes left to finish getting ready. I was still shaking as I left the locker room, still completely stressed out by my close call. I literally thought I wouldn't be able to compete, and over such a small thing!

I was dressed and ready to get on the ice just as our warm-up group was called. On the ice I thought, *Okay, I'm going to see how my Lutz goes.* I did a few triple-triples and felt fine. Mr. Nicks had been right: I'd gotten it back.

After that I just waited and waited. There were so many delays because of the televised broadcast. Two skaters before my turn, I laced up my skates and finished getting ready. As the skater before me bowed and got off the ice, I jumped on, stroking across all those huge rings painted on the rink.

My step-by-step formula kicked in again, a whole bunch of one- or two-word phrases to keep myself going. The most important thing is not to start thinking too far ahead. You'll just freak yourself out. I stayed in the present, the only thing I could control.

And suddenly the present caught up with me. My program began, and I nailed my double axel. Next, on my triple Lutz—triple toe combination, I hung onto my Lutz. But it wasn't strong enough to do a combination, and I fell on the triple toe. I actually just sat on the ice for a second,

✳ *After the Olympics, the U.S. team was invited to the White House for a tour.*

and it was a huge shock. Inside, I was completely crushed. I'd *just* done that combination in warm-up.

But I had to get back to the present moment. I forgot what had happened and thought *only* about what I was doing and what was ahead. It was hard, but I knew it was essential to move on and execute the rest of my program.

The fall had slowed me down a little, so I pushed hard into my next element, the triple flip. After that, the toe and Sal. I knew I had gotten myself back on track, though mentally, it's very tough to recover from a mistake, so it took extra determination. I managed to nail the rest of my elements. By the end, I was breathing very hard. During my footwork I was dying, so tired, but still telling myself, *Push, push, faster, faster.*

I pushed through, but after a mistake like that your heart isn't completely in it. As I landed my other jumps, I built off that momentum, but it had been badly broken up by the fall. Somehow I managed to skate cleanly through the rest of the program.

Once I hit my ending pose I knew it was over. I took a deep breath. This wasn't what I'd hoped for, but I'd tried my best. I took my bows, and stepped off the ice, taking my seat in kiss and cry. My marks were posted a few minutes later, and I knew as soon as I was placed behind Sarah that I wouldn't medal. I was so disappointed.

I felt pretty miserable that night. Once some time passes, the pain lessens, and looking back now, I don't feel so bad. But when you're there you have to say hello to your family and everyone, kind of smile politely through it, and it's really difficult. Everyone had been so focused on the triple-triple that year, I had a really hard time dealing with the fact that I'd missed mine—even if Michelle and Irina had missed theirs, too.

The hotel let us use the club lounge, and a bunch of my family and friends, everyone who had come to watch, came over and had a party. I didn't want to stay that long. I had an impossible time getting to sleep that night, and the next morning I went to the arena for Finale practice. Michelle and I missed our group's early practice because we'd both stayed up so late and needed our rest after all that stress.

My exhibition music, "Hernando's Hideaway," is really energetic and upbeat. I skated well, enjoying it, and at the end of the exhibition we all did a group number, creating the Olympic rings with ribbons.

Disappointed or not, once you're done with the competition you can really enjoy where your hard work has taken you. I spent the rest of my time in Utah hanging around the Olympic Village. The only other event I watched was the gold medal hockey game, which was incredibly exciting because the U.S. team was playing.

And right after the day of my long, the Westins threw me a wonderful dinner party at their house. It was so beautiful and thoughtful, and the food was amazing. Afterward I attended the huge *Sports Illustrated* party in downtown Salt Lake City. We all stayed out until three or four in the morning.

I hadn't won a medal, but I had finally been to the Olympics. I proved to myself that I could get there, and I worked through the enormous challenge of losing a jump. By the time I left Salt Lake City, there was no doubt in my mind that at the end of the next four-year cycle, I wanted to be back on Olympic ice.

Chapter Ten

A NEW CYCLE BEGINS
SUMMER AND FALL 2002

THE WORLD CHAMPIONSHIPS WERE HELD IN Nagano, Japan, that year. It's a pretty quiet event, after the Olympics. Most skaters go, but there was hardly any media attention. Even the skaters are subdued—it's the end of the four-year cycle, and after all the excitement of the Olympics it's hard to be very energetic.

Of course, for me, it was exciting—I was seventeen, and it was my first Worlds. But the overall mood was definitely quiet.

This wasn't helped by the fact that Nagano is a very small village. Traveling there was a mess—we flew all the way to Japan and then had a five-hour bus ride.

But I had a solid qualifying round, placing second to Irina, and was happy with my performance. The day before my short program my mom and I decided to take a walk, just to stay in shape. For some reason I decided to jog instead, which was odd, because I *never* jog—I barely even walk! And yet, somehow, I ended up jogging for a whole hour. My legs were absolutely shot. It was so stupid. Mr. Nicks didn't approve. All he could say was, "Sasha, I can't believe you did that. Very silly, dear."

I couldn't believe it, either, and my legs didn't have time to recover. In my short program I stepped out of my double axel, which dropped me all the way down to fifth, and after that it was hard to rally. I missed two elements in my long, with my legs still completely exhausted, and I placed fourth overall.

It was disappointing for me, as always, not to medal. Especially at my first World Championships, I wanted to do really well. But I guess I was more worn out by the Olympics than I'd thought. And of course the jogging hadn't helped. It was time for a vacation.

So my dad and sister met my mom and me in Hawaii. My best friend Tiffany flew out for three days, too, and she and Natasha and I went to the beach together, got our nails done, and just hung out acting silly and girly. It was so warm and relaxed. Finally I was able to unwind after such an intense season.

And after that, prom! I invited my best friend's boyfriend's best friend Danny—sounds complicated, but we

＊ *Snubaing in Hawaii with Tiffany Stiegler and Natasha*

had a lot of fun. We squished ourselves into a stretch limo with a bunch of other couples, went to dinner by the beach, and then went to the dance, which was held at the Long Beach Aquarium. We walked around looking at all the tanks throughout the dance. It was a really cool place, and much nicer than homecoming had been.

That spring I graduated from Futures High School rather than from my "normal" school. We'd been a really small class, so the ceremony was very intimate and

✳ Getting some sun in Hawaii

personal. Each teacher gave a short speech about their main student, and in the audience it was just our families and close friends. I graduated with straight A's, making the day that much more special.

I was getting a lot of media attention after the Olympics and invitations to various events. The most amazing of all came that summer, when I was asked to perform at the Golden Jubilee to celebrate the Queen of England's fifty-year reign, being held that July. Of course I accepted immediately!

My dad went with me, and we flew British Midways

Airlines. Like the trip to Australia, this flight was so great, I didn't want the flight to end. We had our own chef/steward on board who made food and even a tea party for us—the best food I've ever had on a plane. We were so pampered, it was almost like *we* were royalty.

Once in England we had a three-hour drive. The countryside was gorgeous, like a fairy tale. The Nottingham arena was really nice, too, and being in the show was such an honor for me. The event was hosted by legendary Olympic champion ice dancers Jayne Torvill and Christopher Dean, and they'd invited so many amazing skaters, including my idol Kristi Yamaguchi. For the show itself I did my ribbon program, and didn't get tangled this time.

At the end, we all lined up to meet the queen. She stopped by each of us to shake hands. To me, she said, "Hello." Jayne and Christopher introduced me to her. "So nice to meet you," she said. "Good luck." She was very stately and just as impressive as you'd expect, in a bright red outfit with a huge black hat. Everything was very official, and it was such a big honor and a big deal.

And the whole trip ended perfectly, too: I drove the three hours back to the airport with Kristi. We'd spoken a little at some of the Stars on Ice shows, but this was definitely the most time we'd spent together. She is the nicest, most professional person in the world. I really respect her, her talent, her career, and especially how modest and down-to-earth she is. Someone like Kristi, who's been touring for so many years and is still skating at the same level she was at the Olympics, is such an inspiration for me. And above her professionalism, she's just a really nice, sweet person to everyone.

The Jubilee was a departure from my main tour schedule of the summer: forty-four shows with Champions on Ice. The year before, I had done just a few of the shows; nowhere near this many. It's a really fun show to tour with, and you get to know a lot of skaters in a relaxed, noncompetitive context. But it can also be pretty tiring—especially when we'd take the bus between venues, or when we'd have a show at night and then one the next afternoon. Sometimes it felt like we were just sleeping, driving, and skating!

When I had time off, I was home keeping up with my training schedule. That spring I'd met with Nikoli Morosov, a Russian coach who worked with Tatiana Tarasova in Connecticut. He came to Lake Arrowhead to choreograph my new short and long programs. A month or so later my mom and I went to Connecticut for him to polish the programs, refine them a bit, and put in the final details. Tatiana was there, and she came over to me, giving me directions. "Like this," she'd say in her heavy Russian accent, and I was so impressed with her. She's coached some really amazing skaters, and now she was helping me. I loved the training. It was really intense, a lot of hard work, and a lot more attention than I was used to getting at home.

Back in California I talked to my mom. She had gone to Connecticut with me and had seen how different it was, and how happy I was there. The ice at Aliso Viejo was always crowded and very limited. Mr. Nicks coached many other skaters and taught me for forty-five minutes a day—a third of my ice time. I felt like I was constantly fighting for ice and attention. The time with Tatiana in Connecticut had shown me that I could be working a lot harder, and getting a lot more rink time. But I'd have to move to Connecticut.

I knew my mom didn't want me to move away, and she'd never wanted to divide the family for my skating career. But I told her, "This is where I need to be." I was out of high school, and prepared to go by myself if the family didn't want to move.

We had a lot of discussions about it. My dad's job was pretty flexible at the time, but of course he's from California and has so many friends there. And both of my sets of grandparents live there.

✶ *Tatiana Tarasova and me practicing at the 2003 International Figure Skating Challenge*

Natasha would be switching schools in the fall, anyway, because she'd be starting high school, but again, there was her life to consider, her friends and routine. She was pretty open to the discussion. One day she'd think it was a good idea to move, and the next day she'd want to stay. It was going to affect everyone a lot.

We decided to try it for a year, as a family. That August

we packed everything, putting some stuff in storage and taking a ton with us. I didn't realize how much work moving a house is—we hadn't done it since I was little, and we had so many things to box up! Just packing clothes took forever for me and Natasha. But by Labor Day we'd made the trip to the East Coast. And suddenly, my life had completely changed.

Chapter Eleven

EAST COAST GIRL
THE 2002–2003 SEASON

TRAINING WITH TATIANA WAS MUCH DIFFERENT than it had been with Mr. Nicks. She worked with me every day. Our session was longer, and the ice was practically empty, so rather than pausing and circling around to avoid other skaters, I was working the entire time. From the very beginning the routine was twice as intense.

It was too late in the summer to start serious off-ice training, but she had me do a little running. Almost immediately I started getting stronger.

That season I was skating to "Malagueña" for my short program, and Rachmaninoff's Piano Concerto No. 2, choreographed by Nikoli, for my long. He worked with us for about a month and would skate with me, pushing me to skate stronger. It was such a cool experience, getting all this attention and focus. I'd never realized what having

✳ *Going over my routine in my head*

a full-time, fully involved coach was like!

My first event that fall was the Coalition 9/11 Families fund-raiser, held at Madison Square Garden. I was really honored to be invited, and excited to perform in such a huge venue in New York. I did an easier version of my long program. The whole event was wonderful, pretty small, but with lots of support. Afterward I met Britney

Spears's little sister, Jamie Lynn, and their mom. It wasn't your typical skating event.

In October I went to Daytona Beach, Florida, for the Campbell's competition. It was eighty degrees, but Tatiana was still wearing her fur coat! We were both excited to see how our first official event as skater and coach would go— and it went really well. I was happy with my skate, even though I placed fourth, and I focused on improving for the bigger competitions coming up.

Right around my eighteenth birthday I was asked to open the rink at Rockefeller Center in New York City, on the *Today* show. It was early in the morning, and cold—two things I don't enjoy, but meeting Matt Lauer was fun. And skating there is amazing because you look up and you're just surrounded by skyscrapers.

Skate Canada was next, and I wasn't in top form—but no one else skated well, either. Early in the season everyone's still getting in shape—if we were perfect in October, by March we'd be dead! So I wasn't perfect, but I beat the competition and took home the gold medal, which, of course, is always nice.

Then I went to Trophée Lalique and won the gold there, too. The Lalique prize is a glass medal and a really beautiful crystal trophy. So I was very excited to take it home, and also was thrilled to have qualified for my first Grand Prix final.

✳ *At the 2002 Skate Canada, with Fumie Suguri and Victoria Volchkova*

My last Grand Prix that year was the Cup of Russia. I landed six clean triples, and although I ended up finishing second to Russian Victoria Volchkova, I was really happy with my performance. The event was in Moscow, and Tatiana took me to her favorite restaurant called Café Pushkin. It's a gorgeous place, with lots of detailed paintings on the walls, like a museum. And it was the best food I've ever had in Russia.

Later that month I was invited back to New York

※ In the Thanksgiving Day Parade. It was so cold out there!

City, this time for the Macy's Thanksgiving Day Parade. I stood on the Statue of Liberty float with a runner from the 1960 Olympics and had the most amazing time. It was freezing cold, of course, and even with my usual fifty layers of thermal clothing I was shivering. The wind channeled right down the street, blasting us the whole way. But you could see people watching from their windows along the street, and the sidewalks were completely packed. Everyone was cheering. It was incredible. Afterward, there was a great party with a whole table of different desserts—definitely worth freezing for—and I got to

✳ *Spinning at the Crest competition*

meet Justin Guarini from *American Idol*, and Ashanti, and lots of other celebrities.

For Thanksgiving, the whole family came to New York City and we all went out to dinner. My schedule was so hectic then, it was really nice to have everyone together.

Right after that I did the Sears Figure Skating Open, performing my brand-new artistic *Romeo and Juliet* program. This was really just a made-for-television event, so I wasn't overly concerned. That was one of the reasons that I decided to go without my mom this time. It was the first competition I went to without her, and also the first time I got 6.0s from the judges. That was such an amazing moment—I'd finally gotten a perfect score. I was so excited about that, and about getting first place.

I competed in one more event before the 2003 Nationals, the International Figure Skating Challenge, in Auburn Hills, Michigan. I skated really, really well there, landed six triples, and stepped out of a seventh. I was very proud of that program, and took the gold again. The season was going well, and I was feeling good about Nationals.

That first winter in Connecticut was fun—at first. We weren't used to snow, and for a while we thought, *Oh, this is so nice*, but it kept being cold and it kept snowing, and before I knew it I'd bought three or four coats! My whole family was shocked at how cold it always was.

✳ *A triple Lutz, midair, at the International Figure Skating Challenge*

After a quiet Christmas at home, it was time to get ready for the 2003 Nationals, being held in Dallas. Michelle had skipped the Grand Prix events, so there was some attention on how she would perform. I was determined to do well, and put a lot of pressure on myself before I even got there.

I had a pretty good short. I put my foot down on my combination, and all the judges placed me second. I thought, *That was stupid, but oh well. I'm in the top three and that's all that matters. The long is where I really need to execute.*

I remember being so nervous before my long program, giving my mom a hug at the final checkpoint, making my way downstairs on my own. I went through my warm-up, and everything was fine. And the beginning of my program was strong—I double-footed my triple-triple, but then cleanly landed three more triples.

Wow, you did all your most difficult elements, I thought. *The rest is easy—you really only need one triple here, not two.* And in that moment, when I stopped to question myself, I changed my timing. I went for just the triple toe instead of the combination. Because I had hesitated, I got really crooked, and I fell.

I was in complete shock, devastated. Everything had been going so well! The audience was surprised, too, and let out a big "Ohhhh."

When you fall on the ice, it's like everything inside you falls too. It's really hard to pull yourself back up. And that day I didn't do a very good job of pulling it together. I was crying when I got off the ice, crying in my press conference. It was so hard. I'd placed third, but I wasn't disappointed that I wasn't second, I just cared that I'd completely blown an opportunity to skate my best at Nationals. I'd put too much pressure on myself, but even worse, I didn't go with it. You have to trust your body, you can't hesitate or question yourself. I'd let my mind wander, and it ruined my performance.

Tatiana could be a very comforting coach in a situation like this. In the beginning she was much more involved than Mr. Nicks had been, always there and a part of everything, guiding me, saying, "You need to rest now" or, "I want you to run for ten minutes." I definitely felt like I was in good hands. At competitions she was always with me, even in the locker room, which was actually kind of weird and made me a little more nervous at first. But her intentions were good, and she always wanted to be there to protect me. While Mr. Nicks had been sort of formal and distant, Tatiana was like a devoted Russian grandma.

After Nationals it took me a while to bounce back. I went out to California to visit my friends, but even there

✳ *The 2003 Nationals exhibition skate*

it was hard to see people. After you don't skate well, you're so busy dealing with your own disappointment, you just want to pretend it never happened, but of course everyone saw it on TV. I stopped by my old rink and my favorite places, just trying to relax.

A few weeks later I did a fashion shoot for *Seventeen* magazine. Normally I'd have been really excited about this, but I was so sick that day, I felt absolutely terrible. I had orange juice, my mom went to get tea, and the magazine people brought a heater out onto the ice to keep me warm while I posed in different outfits with my skates on. I was very fussed over, but it was still a tough shoot. When the pictures came back and looked terrific, I was so happy!

I also did some ads for Citizen Watch around this time. We shot a commercial after Worlds that year, during a break in my tour schedule. It was one of my first big deals, and the shoot was so professional, with so many people, just done really, really well. Everything was great—the catered lunch, the makeup, the wardrobe, the cappuccino delivery. I was really starting to like this modeling stuff.

But back in the world of competing, it was time to concentrate again. The Grand Prix Final in Saint Petersburg was my first event after Nationals. Tatiana, my mom, and I flew to Paris first so I could start getting used to the time change without having to spend an extra week in Russia. We found a rink to train in, so during the day I skated, and at night we had time to walk around and enjoy being in Paris. A few days later my sister and dad came, and my grandparents happened to be there on a trip of their own. It was nice having everyone there, because I could get work done and also have a nice time in Paris with my family. It made it feel more like a vacation instead of a stressed-out preparation week.

Then we flew to Saint Petersburg for my first Grand Prix final. It was a really cool event, for a lot of reasons, and especially because we did everything exactly the same way, every day. We'd practice in a particular order, then rest, then perform, Thursday through Saturday. You saw the same people in the locker room when you got ready, the same people finishing their programs on the ice before you went on, the same people waiting to perform after you. It was like that movie *Groundhog Day*: After a while, things were almost eerily familiar. I kind of enjoyed the routine, because usually competitions are so frenzied and unpredictable.

Plus, everything's nicer at a Grand Prix final—the hotel, the food. We didn't have time to tour Saint Petersburg, but I really enjoyed the whole event.

It was a very small competition, with just the six finalists from each category, and I was the only American competitor there. Because of that they hadn't sent a team doctor along, or a team leader. But Linda Leaver, who was an American judge to the event, filled the role of team leader and made me feel very comfortable.

I did a great short, and I was really excited because I beat Irina Slutskaya. We didn't think I'd be able to beat a Russian skater in Russia; we'd thought I wouldn't get the marks, and on top of that, she was the current world champion.

Then during the long program, held later that day, I made a few mistakes and placed second. It was disappointing, but I still had another long the next day—worth fifty percent of my total score. That was the time to make it happen, I kept telling myself.

So on Saturday I skated fifth and Irina was on right after me. No one was excellent that year. It just wasn't the strongest final—after an Olympic year, no one's usually at their peak performance level. But I had been training really hard with Tatiana and was much stronger than I'd ever been. On the ice I was very determined, thinking about each jump, fighting for every landing. I made one mistake but still skated really well. As I nailed my last triple-double, I pushed faster, radiant and smiling, feeling like, *Yes. That was good.*

Irina made some mistakes after me, and I had straight

first places from all the judges. I couldn't believe how well my first Grand Prix final had turned out! I was the first American to win the gold medal at a final since Tara Lipinski in 1998. They gave me a huge trophy, a medal, and flowers, and as I stood on the podium listening to the U.S. National Anthem, with Russian skaters on either side of me, I felt so proud. The Russians won all the other events, so to represent the U.S. with a win was huge for me.

I was ecstatic. Nationals had been such a low—I'd even been crying during my exhibition skate at Nationals! And now I felt great, like I was on top of the world. You really do feel just as good as your last competition, so it was beyond satisfying to have such a good performance late in the season. The exhibition skate was really fun, and the audience was great. It went on for a while—I remember Evgeny Plushenko did a twelve-minute encore.

For the final banquet they asked me to give a short welcoming speech, so I nervously made my way to the mic and said something like, "Thank you for making this such a wonderful event. It's an honor to compete with the best skaters in the world. This has been a wonderful experience for me, and a great competition, and I'm so grateful to the Russian people for being so supportive and being such great hosts."

I was elated, and relieved, and so ready for some down

time—except there was no time; I still had to focus. The Worlds were right around the corner, and this year they were being held in Washington, D.C. Anytime a competition is in America, it's important because of all the media attention. So this Worlds felt completely different from how it had the year before, in Nagano. There was a ton of attention, banners being hung all around the city.

For me, Worlds was good and bad. I practiced well, my triple-triple was strong, and I completed my first clean long program ever in the qualifying round—a big first for me. Unfortunately, I didn't get the marks, and was only third, but I was so happy to have landed all seven triples.

Then, in the short I missed my timing and fell on my flip, but I got right back up and was still on fire. I just went numb about the fall, and moved into my next elements with all my strength. Great layback, great double axel—I turned the disappointment into energy for the rest of the program. At the end, I still got a standing ovation because everyone could see how much energy I had, finishing the program so strongly.

But I was still placed too low to win. I had come in thinking, *I want to win Worlds*, but after the short, I knew it couldn't happen.

I cried and cried that night. Everyone was trying to get

me to stop, but I was so emotional. My mom and Tatiana and everyone kept saying, "Stop it! Don't emotionally drain yourself! Save it for tomorrow!" But I was heartbroken.

It was unbelievable how nervous I was for the long program. We had something like ten hours between practice and the competition, a whole day to worry and dwell on it. I tried to calm down, rested a little, took a shower and washed my hair. Then I went to Tatiana's room to talk to her about the program, and she cried, "Why did you wash your hair?! Don't blow-dry it!" It's this superstition that you're not supposed to wash (or blow-dry) your hair the day of a competition, and she obviously was taking it very seriously! So I let my hair air-dry.

And in the end, it didn't seem to bring me any bad luck. I skated well, and I met another goal: landing a triple-triple for the first time in competition. Everyone was, like, whoa, did you see that? But again I made a mistake on my triple toe. I made a lot of mistakes on that jump that year. It's always at the end of the program, and I'm always tired by the time I get to it. I still had six clean triples and I placed third in the long—but fourth overall.

Inside, I was, like, *I can't believe it. I'm fourth* again. But by then, another part of me was saying, *Whatever. Stop thinking about it.* I just kind of turned it off, and it was the best way to deal with it. If you start thinking about how things *could* have gone, what you *could* have done, you just make yourself so upset. I'd done that before and had just made myself feel worse. Now I don't dwell on things. I make a new plan of action, and use the fall or the mistake as motivation. You can turn anything into positive energy.

So on tour that summer I got into great shape, skating really well every night. That's another thing I've learned. I used to be a terrible show skater. I couldn't deal with not having a warm-up; in a show, you just get on and perform cold, but without that five minutes of preparation, I never felt ready. That year I learned to become a consistent show skater, learned what it took to stay in shape, started eating healthier, doing all my core exercises every day, really working hard even though a lot of people slack off on tour. I was able to turn the disappointment into something productive. I could hit everything solidly in my exhibition program.

And I needed a real vacation, so my friend Christie Baca and I decided to go to Cancún, Mexico—just the two of us. It was another big step, going on vacation on my own. My mom used to be *so* protective of me—lots of, "Where are you? What are you doing?" As I've gotten older she's realized I'm very responsible and really pretty conservative. She knows I make smart decisions. So by then I was eighteen and she trusted me to go to Cancún. It's not like we did anything crazy. We went to a different club or disco every night, then slept in late every day. But the hours in between were all spent lying by the pool, Jet Skiing, swimming with dolphins (which was *so* fun), visiting ancient Mayan ruins, scuba diving, seeing the wildlife. And we ate a lot of limes—they're really good there, and I became a little obsessed.

When I got home, Tatiana was really upset with me. "You're too skinny!" she cried. We'd been so busy in Mexico, we'd only had time to eat, like, one meal a day. I usually eat a lot of food, so I probably did lose about four pounds while I was there.

So we got back into my intense program right away, running, weights, meeting with my off-ice coach for jumping practice.

I used the summer to focus and get stronger. It was my first off-season with Tatiana, so she put me on a full off-ice training schedule, with running and weight lifting. I was eating really well and felt stronger than ever.

Tatiana had brought some music from Russia, *Swan Lake*, to consider for my new short program. After listening to it, we thought it might actually make a better long. I'd never considered using *Swan Lake* for a program, because, like *Carmen*, it's a very popular piece. But the cuts she brought were really unusual and beautiful, so we set the program and it turned out really well. After fruitlessly searching through tons of other possible choices, we kept "Malagueña" for my short.

The dress was a little more of a struggle. Tatiana and I have very different taste in costumes, and she wanted me to be a full-out swan for this one, feathers everywhere. My taste in costumes is much more conservative, so I went ahead and had the dress made by a Canadian designer, without the suggested feathers on my shoulders or in my hair. When Tatiana first saw the dress, she said, "Oh! Let me take that and fix it for you! There are no feathers!" We compromised.

And suddenly, summer was over. I was stronger than ever, and ready for the new season to begin.

Chapter Twelve

HITTING MY STRIDE
2003 TO 2004

A YEAR HAD GONE BY, AND IT LOOKED LIKE WE were on the East Coast to stay for a while longer. Natasha started school that fall at the highly regarded Miss Porter's School, in Farmington, Connecticut, near our new house in Avon. I especially liked being so close to New York City, one of my favorite cities.

In fact, my first event of the 2003–2004 season was in New York, back at Madison Square Garden, for the Campbell's Classic Invitational. It was a Pro Am, a made-for-TV event, but it was my first event of the year, and my first time skating against the top six ladies in the world. So of course I was really nervous! All my experience was starting to pay off, though. I stayed in the present, stayed focused. I skated last, and each element was solid. At the end I got a standing ovation—in Madison Square Garden!

Even more amazing, I'd beaten Michelle Kwan for the first time. It was quite a way to start a season.

I was on a real high that night. We enjoyed the rest of the weekend in the city, and then went home to train for Skate America.

That's when I began to take a little of the nervousness out of competition and just enjoy it. For once I felt like I was ahead of the other skaters, because I was so strong and prepared. I just told myself, *This isn't too important; it'll be easy. I'm going to enjoy this, just do what I've done a million times in practice.*

As soon as we got to the town in Pennsylvania where the event was held, I noticed something unusual. There were banners of my picture all over town! The attention made me feel even more excited to be there.

When you can skate and be free and relaxed, it makes a huge difference. I held on to my positive, relaxed attitude. I just skated, just let go and let my body do what it knew how to do, and I nailed all of my elements. The audience gave me a standing ovation after both my short and long programs, and I placed first!

The next day was both the exhibition skate and my birthday. I performed really well, and then I took a limo that drove me up to New York City. We had dinner at this amazing French-Mediterranean restaurant, Picholine. Our waiter recognized me and gave us an extra course,

✳ *My short program at Skate Canada*

extra attention, and lots of dessert. It was a really special birthday. We took the next day off to go shopping, and then I was on the *Today* show the day after that.

My season was packed that year. The day after the *Today* show I was back in Connecticut training, and that night, I flew to Skate Canada.

My short was better than it had been at Skate America, and my long was okay. I didn't do any combinations, but I wasn't too upset about it, and my scores were high enough that I took home the gold for the third time in three events. I remember those weeks as hectic and happy, really pleased with how well I was skating.

So I felt good going to Trophée Lalique, getting there the weekend before, to adjust to the time difference and practice. My short was clean, and I was placed first. And then that night I guess all the running around caught up with me. I started feeling really sick. I seemed to be coming down with the flu, and of course the timing was terrible. I knew the long was going to be so much harder if I was sick and had no energy. So I stayed in bed the whole next day, going to the ice briefly to just practice one of each jump.

When you're competing in back-to-back events, you aren't training. You're practicing, maintaining, but the big work gets done only when you have a couple of weeks to train. So not only was I feeling sick, I was starting to get weaker, not having the time to train in my normal way. So I had to be smart, and careful. I took myself through a mild warm-up, listening to my body. I was still exhausted, but I remember looking at the Lalique prize—that gorgeous crystal trophy—and thinking, *I want another one of those!* The desire helped me be determined and focused. During the long I touched down on a double axel, and otherwise skated very well. The next day I had a second beautiful Lalique trophy for the mantel back home, and a full-blown case of the flu.

At this point I did sort of wonder if I'd overbooked my season. There were a lot of events I just couldn't pass up, and months before, when I'd scheduled everything, it had all seemed perfectly reasonable. Even with a runny nose and high fever, I knew I couldn't skip my next show: Scott Hamilton's cancer fund-raising event in Cleveland, in honor of Helen McLoraine, a benefactor of Scott's skating (and mine).

Scott's show is really well done, and even though I was worn out from the lapse in training and all the time-zone changes I'd been through, I was honored to be a part of it. Afterward, my mom and I met Dad and Natasha in Miami for three days to try to rest. And then, bam, it was time to start training for my Pro Am in Detroit in a week.

This was the first year I was consistently doing a lot of clean run-throughs, which gave me a lot of confidence. Even tired, I practiced well. But only having one week to get ready for the ABC Pro Am was tough. I expected to skate well, but I missed my first jump. Not only was it the first time I'd fallen all season, I managed to fall in a huge puddle. My legs were soaked, and cold. I was just in shock, thinking, *How did I miss that jump?* And I'm sorry to say that I kind of shut down after that. I missed the next jump, stepped out of another, and came off the ice dripping wet, in a daze, and miserable.

I was third, and worse, I'd skated absolutely terribly—one of the worst performances of my life. I was really disappointed and shocked, but I reminded myself, *Hey, it's a Pro Am. You want to present yourself in the best light every time you skate, but you have to keep perspective.*

The really frustrating thing about that event was that my mom and I couldn't get home from it. There was a huge snowstorm, and all the airports on the East Coast were shutting down. We managed to fly to Washington, D.C., and then they cancelled all flights to Connecticut, so we were stuck again. At that point, we were desperate to get back to Connecticut and we considered renting a car to drive to another airport, but instead we somehow got put on the train. We'd left at seven o'clock that morning and finally got home at midnight. I'd decided my bad performance wasn't the end of the world, but after all the travel and frustration, I was completely worn out.

But still, there was no time to relax. I had Sunday to rest, then went back to training that Monday, and left that Wednesday for my Grand Prix Final. It was held in Colorado Springs—as if things weren't going to be tough already, I'd also have to deal with skating at a higher altitude.

Tatiana and I started having some troubles around this time. She had some health concerns, both of her own and her mom's, and at competitions we weren't communicating well. At the Grand Prix final I lost my timing on my Lutz. I missed it in the short, and I was crying and really upset. Unfortunately, Tatiana was also very upset, which didn't help.

So I had to pull myself together for the long, and it was really difficult. I got through my first three jumps, got the Lutz back, did my flip and loop, but again—my triple toe. It was actually a good jump, but I just slipped off my landing and sat down at the end. Then I missed the next flip. I just wasn't in good enough shape for the altitude, and to make matters even worse, I'd had some back spasms earlier that day. I tried, I put out my best effort, but there was way too much going on! It was nice to still be second place

✳ *Practicing at the 2003 Grand Prix Final in Colorado Springs*

at the final, and I was glad that my best efforts to muddle through the difficulties had gotten me somewhere. But it was a tough, tough time.

After that I was finally able to take some time off. But things with Tatiana still weren't going very well. My parents had talked to Robin Wagner, the coach who had taken Sarah Hughes to the Olympics. She was available to take on a student, and agreed to take me on. We arranged a meeting just a few days before Christmas.

It was pretty awkward. We met at my house, and it was weird because I'd always known her as my competitor's coach. She was one of those people I'd say hi to in passing, but she was, you know, on the other side.

But I'd definitely noticed and admired how supportive and dedicated to Sarah she was. We talked a little bit, then started working together at the rink two days before Christmas. I saw how she trained, she saw how I worked. We got along very well. I could really talk to her and get to know her. She was sweet and supportive, which I desperately needed at that time.

New Year's is always quiet for me because Nationals is around the corner. My family had come out from California, and we baked and spent time together. But my mind was preoccupied with getting a new coach, so it was really hectic, not feeling the most holiday spirit. And New

Year's Eve is just like any other night for me—I usually go to bed around ten, especially since I have to leave a couple of days later for Nationals.

Robin trained me every day for the two weeks before Nationals. It was too hard for me to travel and train at the same time, so she drove three and a half hours each way from her home on Long Island. I couldn't believe how much effort she took with me.

We had just a few days left. I had a new coach, I had a huge event coming up, and I had last year's disappointing Nationals to make up for. It wasn't going to be easy.

Chapter Thirteen

A NEW CHAPTER BEGINS
2004

WE GOT TO ATLANTA AND IMMEDIATELY CHECKED into a different hotel from the other competitors'. Once you reach a certain level competitively, it's just too hard to stay in the official hotel. You can't get any privacy or rest; it's too crazy. This was my first year at that level, and the change was really good for me. It felt like, *Okay, I'm at a hotel and relaxing,* instead of, *Yikes, I'm at a major skating event!*

I wasn't doing any off-ice training then, but I was feeling stronger. Robin was very calm and reassuring. I felt good.

My short was great: well executed, really strong. I had to stay late that night to be interviewed by the media after the event. It was lucky I had a day in between that and the long program, because after all the attention, I was exhausted.

✳ *My new coach, Robin Wagner, with me, Dad, and Mom*

My mom and Robin were not sure why I was so tired, and I had no idea, either.

Two days later I had more energy for the long, but I still felt tired. I over-warmed up, which was a silly mistake since I had to skate first. A five-minute warm-up followed by a four-minute program—basically I was doing a nine-minute program. Things were going really well until the middle. I started to feel exhausted, and that's when mistakes happen. I missed my triple toe. It was so,

✳ *My long program at the 2004 Nationals—the* Swan Lake *dress,
without too many feathers*

so disappointing. In practice, I never miss it!

But I finished the rest of the program strong—better than the year before, and winning the silver medal. I didn't let myself get upset like I had in Dallas. Off the ice, Robin and I were positive. There was next year; we had time to figure out what I needed to do to skate well. I sort of just shrugged my shoulders and moved on.

And the next day I was able to skate a great exhibition—the year before, I'd been so upset, even my exhibition had been terrible. Above all, it was good to have Robin on my side. She was very focused and had a plan: We're going to train, we're going to get ready for Worlds. She turned my disappointment into motivation, made it something positive.

Back home we had to figure out a training schedule. The commute was terrible between Connecticut and New Jersey, and neither of us could handle it every day. Splitting up the week sort of made sense, but still meant one of us would be exhausted every time we met. So out of incredible generosity, Robin offered for me to stay with her and her husband, Jerry, at their house. I had the whole second floor to myself, a great bedroom, a TV, everything.

We still had to drive a lot, out to New Jersey, and the three-hour commute every day was pretty hard. We left at 8:00 in the morning and got home at 8:30 or 9:00 every night. But we got into a routine. Every morning we

✳ *With my silver medal and flowers at Nationals*

stopped at Starbucks, and every evening after practice we went to the gym and out to dinner. By the time we got home all we had to do was go to bed.

Robin would get on the ice and skate with me, showing me takeoffs or spins. If I was going too slow she'd skate alongside me and tell me to get going. Nikoli was the only other coach I'd had who'd done this, and to have that back again was great. It's just different to have someone out there with you rather than watching from the boards.

By March we'd really gotten to know each other, what with spending twelve hours a day together and planning a new and improved long program. We were going to New York City, meeting with the designers Badgley Mischka, having dinner, finding new blades. I soon knew Robin better than I'd known any of my other coaches.

Before Worlds we started working on my new show program, which was set to dialogue and music from the movie soundtrack of *My Fair Lady*. It's my favorite movie, and I adore Audrey Hepburn, so it was a really fun program to choreograph. Robin brought music in and we decided to make it theatrical and start with a coat over my dress, showing the transformation of Eliza Doolittle through the course of the program. It was nice to work on that as a change of pace before Worlds.

I was also getting to know the New York City area better and was really enjoying spending time there.

Then, all of a sudden, it was time to leave for Worlds. We went to Germany a couple of days early to get used to the time difference, as usual. I wanted to be really careful to pace myself through the qualifying round, short, and then long programs. It takes a lot of endurance to concentrate on your programs *and* deal with the media. And I never used to have enough stamina to make it through a competition without feeling really, really tired. So we were very focused on my strength and energy.

Everything was going well, and then right before the qualifying rounds, I lost my triple loop. I couldn't believe this was happening! And it wasn't like I was stepping out of it or landing inconsistently; I'd completely lost it, and couldn't get it back.

I was just going nuts. Robin calmed me down, promising I'd have it back by Saturday, reminding me that I didn't need it for my qualifying program, suggesting that I do a spiral instead.

I calmed down, and of course it turned out she was right. I placed first in the qualifying group without my loop.

In my short program the next day I was just on fire. The judges even gave me a few 6.0s, and everyone was amazed at how well I'd skated. To be in first after qualifying and after the short was so exciting. I was on top of the world.

I was still being careful to save my energy, and on the last day I got my loop back like Robin had promised—

✳ *Very nervous and being coached by Robin Wagner at Worlds in Germany, 2004*

✳ *A Charlotte in my short program at Worlds. You have to be really balanced for this move!*

after watching a ton of videos of myself landing it.

As always, I was incredibly nervous before my long program. At every competition, you learn something about yourself as a skater, and at that one I learned even more how important it is to let your body go when you skate. I was shaky and tentative during that program, and I wasn't able to just let it happen. There are so many things you need to do to be strong and handle the pressure, but when you're skating, you have to let your skating come out—you can't force it. I completed all of my elements, but missed the takeoff on my last Sal, doing a double instead. I ended up placing second.

I was upset for a couple of hours, but I forced myself to not dwell on it. I accepted my silver medal gladly—after all, I had just won my first World medal!—and moved on.

Just a few days later, I left for the Champions on Ice tour. It was my first year completely on my own, though of course I had lots of good friends in the show, including Johnny Weir and Timmy Goebel. We started rehearsals, and I got my new dresses. The *My Fair Lady* outfit was a beautifully beaded white dress with a sparkling tiara, just like Audrey Hepburn wore in the movie. I loved it.

I came home from Germany for half a day, unpacked and packed again, then set off on the six-hour drive to

✳ The podium at Worlds—me with my silver, Shizuka Arakawa with the gold, and Michelle Kwan with the bronze

the rehearsals for Champions on Ice. After a few days of rehearsals, we had a dress rehearsal, then a charity show, then seven straight shows, a day to train, then the Marshalls Challenge (a Pro Am), then back on tour. We worked straight through for three weeks. It was really difficult to be skating so much after we'd worked so hard for Worlds, and when the season was officially over. I was going to see the tour's physical therapist, Eric Lang, every day. My body would have fallen apart without him!

Robin came to a couple of the Champions shows to train me for the Marshalls. That day, I did my long program during the show practice because there wasn't any other free time. I had no idea what kind of performance I would give at the Pro Am the next day, but all the skaters were in the same situation. We all hadn't trained since

✳ *Rudy Galindo, Nicole Bobek, and me in our amazing costumes for Champions on Ice*

✳ *Johnny Weir and I do our "prom pose" at the 2004 Worlds closing banquet*

※ *A stop on the tour in Seattle, right after the Olympics. Rented a boat with Shae-Lynn Bourne, Timmy Goebel, and Peter Tchernyshev.*

before Worlds, and we were very run down from traveling and doing shows. The season was over, so I wasn't really nervous, and the whole event was low key compared to Worlds. But an event like that is also your last chance to "show 'em what you've got," so to speak, before everyone goes home for the summer.

For the competition Robin suggested I try something new. "Just skate and let it happen," she told me, and I did.

It ended up being the best event of the whole season. I landed all seven triples, skating even better than I had at the Campbell's, and I won! It felt so great to end the season on such a high note.

In June I took some time off and went to Italy with my family for a few weeks. And then came my traveling period. My family had decided to move to New York City, so they ended the lease on our house in Connecticut and began the endless search for the perfect apartment in Manhattan. I was excited to move to the city, and to be so much closer to my training in New Jersey. I stayed with my aunt for a while, then with friends, then with other friends. It was pretty unsettled, but there's so much great shopping and so many good restaurants in New York—two things I love!—and having my family and my coach

✳ *The best gelato place in Rome. I'm fluent in ice cream!*

*✳ Natasha told us to point at this fountain in Italy. Not sure why . . .
she's artistic.*

nearby made all the upheaval worthwhile.

And of course I was excited to be moving toward
another season. I knew the pressure would really start,
as we were moving closer to the 2006 Olympics. With
Robin's help, I'd be training for that goal—and for all
the other challenges in between.

Chapter Fourteen

COMING FULL CIRCLE:
THE 2004–2005 SEASON BEGINS

LATE SUMMER AND FALL OF 2004 WERE COMPLETELY crazy. My family was still traveling a lot, going back and forth from Southern California, our Sun Valley trip in Idaho, New York City, New Jersey, and Connecticut.

For a while we rented an apartment in New Jersey, close to where I was training with Robin. It was a fun place to live—there were lots of shops in our apartment complex, and nearby I could go running along the Hudson River with incredible views of New York City.

With New York right there, we visited often, trying new restaurants and shopping. But it wasn't until late September that we were actually able to move into our new apartment near Lincoln Center in Manhattan. I could look out my window and see New Jersey, now from the other side of the Hudson River.

Natasha went back to Miss Porter's for the new school year, and she started running with the cross-country team. My parents and I would drive up most weekends to visit her and watch her run. She's really good!

My skating was going okay, but various problems made my summer difficult and I wasn't very prepared for the upcoming season. At my first event, the Campbell's Classic, I knew I wasn't in peak form. I went out and skated all right, but it wasn't a great performance. I still had a lot of work ahead of me.

But later that month, about a week before Skate America, my first Grand Prix event, my back started hurting again. One day it just hurt a little bit, but the next day it was worse. By the third day I knew I needed to take action. My old back injury had definitely taught me not to wait, but to fix problems immediately.

So I flew out to Chicago to see my doctor, and I called off competing at Skate America and my other Grand Prix appearances. I was disappointed to miss those events, but within just a few weeks of physical therapy and being careful, my back felt completely better.

My break was worth the disappointment, and besides, the end of the season is the most important time. To risk seriously injuring myself getting through October and November would have been crazy—I knew I really needed to be healthy for the last months of the season, to do well in Nationals and Worlds.

That fall I also started skating in New York City, at the rink in Chelsea Piers. Robin and I worked there together during the week, and afterward I was able to take a quick walk to my physical therapist and Pilates classes. My jumps came back after a short time off, and we threw ourselves into making my new Nutcracker program the best it could be.

During my free time, my parents and I explored the city and tried new restaurants—there are so many good ones in New York!—and for my birthday my Babba came to visit. We all went out to a seafood restaurant in SoHo on Halloween night, though we left before the Greenwich Village Halloween Parade began. We saw them setting up for it, though, and it looked like a big deal!

Our apartment was really close to Central Park, so I started running there a few times a week. My mom and I picked out new furniture in SoHo and saw movies at the theater right next to our apartment. After so many years of visiting New York, it was so exciting to actually live there! Every time we visited Natasha in Connecticut we marveled at how we'd ever survived living in such a quiet, rural environment.

On the ice I was still working on my new program, though it wasn't coming together the way I'd hoped. I was having a lot of problems with the costume, too. We just couldn't seem to find the right designer and fit, and with my first performance in over a month coming up at the Marshalls World Cup, I needed a plan, quickly.

I still didn't have new dresses, so I decided to wear my *Swan Lake* costume, which was white and simple enough to look like the nightgown Clara wears in *The Nutcracker*.

Most of all, I needed to concentrate on my skating. All summer and fall I'd been trying new training techniques, on and off the ice, and now it seemed I'd lost a lot of my timing. My jumps were off, and while everyone was giving me advice and tips, I still couldn't get them right.

When we traveled to Detroit for the Marshalls Pro Am the first week of December, things got even worse. First, the airline lost my luggage—including my skates! At first we thought they'd be on the next flight, but when they hadn't shown up *six* incoming flights later, I really started to panic. It's not like you can just go out and get another pair of skates. Especially in a competition, your boots and blades have to be just right. Any last-minute changes can be disastrous.

By midnight, my luggage finally showed up at the hotel. I'd missed that day's practice, but I was able to practice the next day and calm my nerves. Unfortunately, I still wasn't in the shape I needed to be in. I hadn't been ready at all during the season; I hadn't been able to get to that turning point where everything falls into place.

My program at the Pro Am was really disappointing. I fell on three jumps, and as soon as it was over I knew—something had to change. I had to get my timing back; I had to get to that turning point. And I had to do it soon, because Nationals was just over a month away.

On top of everything else, my family and I were all growing increasingly homesick for California. As much as we all loved New York, it wasn't home. After the Pro Am I went to Washington, D.C., to concentrate on my jumps. I studied lots of videotapes and worked on my own. I visited Michael Weiss and his family, and skated with them and with other elite athletes.

I also spent some time just watching tapes of my own jumps, without anyone telling me what to do or giving me advice. That really helped me to take charge of my skating again.

That trip gave me time to think about how homesick I was, and how things weren't working out the way I'd hoped they would in New York. When I got back I talked to Robin about everything. She was really supportive—she was always an incredibly supportive coach—but it just wasn't coming together.

So with a few weeks to go before Nationals, I decided

to try going back to California. Of course this was another big upheaval for the whole family—we stayed with friends, then finally rented an apartment, and our lives were completely up in the air for a while. Natasha came with us, on Christmas break from school, and we did our best to settle in quickly.

As soon as I got back to Orange County, my skating improved. I started training with Mr. Nicks again. I'd gained so much from training with Tatiana and Robin, grown so

✳ *2005 U.S. Nationals—at practice with Mr. Nicks*

much as a person, and learned so much about what you need to approach competitions physically and mentally. Back with Mr. Nicks, things were familiar and smooth. The tremendous amount of experience I'd had since I'd last trained with him really added to our work together.

Mr. Nicks is a really great coach to direct me, and he always forces me to be unique and do my own moves. He has an incredible eye for a program. And he's so supportive, helping me build confidence in my own skating. As my practices became more consistent, I grew even more self-assured, and soon it felt like everything was finally falling into place.

Even with so much going on, I still needed to find two new competition dresses. Time was really running out, but right before Christmas we managed to find a designer. It was my last shot at finding new dresses, so I was pretty nervous.

All the commotion left very little time for any Christmas celebrations. The week before we still had no tree, no presents, no apartment. But being back in California, near our family, was wonderful. We'd all wanted to come back eventually, and it felt great to be home.

Finally we found some time to run around buying presents and getting ready for the holiday. Our new apartment was right on the beach, and though it wasn't quite swimsuit weather, it was so much warmer than New York. My mom and I went to the salon together and got pedicures with little flowers painted on our toes. We were so excited to be able to wear sandals again, and that seemed like the best way to celebrate!

My Babba came to visit, and on Christmas we all went out to dinner with my dad's family. We ate at a delicious Moroccan restaurant and had a wonderful time.

Being back in California was great for all of us. We visited with our friends, going to a lot of dinner parties and holiday parties. Even the little things, like my favorite frozen yogurt place (Golden Spoon—the best!), felt familiar and comforting. It was just so good to be home again.

On New Year's Eve I went out to dinner with my mom and her friends, then to a friend's party to count down to midnight. I caught up with my friend and fellow skater Evan Lysacek and had a great time ringing in 2005.

Since we'd gotten back to California, I'd been steadily training, preparing, going to fittings for the dresses, settling in to our new apartment, running errands. Thank goodness, the meeting with the dressmaker before Christmas had gone well, and she'd worked basically day and night for three weeks on my dresses. I now had a costume for my short program and another almost done for my long.

Chapter Fifteen

2005 NATIONALS

RIGHT AFTER NEW YEAR'S, NATASHA WENT BACK TO school in Connecticut, and that same week I had a little mock competition at my rink to get ready for Nationals.

Mr. Nicks suggested I have a practice event, just like we used to. I remembered it being a very good way to prepare for a competition. So I came in one night, did a five-minute warm-up, and performed my short program in my new dress.

By the week before Nationals I was starting to get nervous, but my practices were still nice and solid. It was such a rush to feel confident on the ice again, to have beautiful dresses finally coming together, to be home. It had been a long time since I'd skated well, or had costumes! I could hardly believe how smoothly things were going.

The Sunday before we left, I had my new long-program dress and was able to practice in it on Monday. After a quick refitting, we were ready to go.

We left for Portland, Oregon, the Tuesday before Nationals. Mr. Nicks and my mom came with me, and my dad and grandma came out to meet us later. As soon as we got there, I did my interview with ABC, got dinner, and checked in to the hotel.

We had most of Wednesday to relax and shop, walking around Portland (which was really cold and rainy compared to California!). That evening I went to practice my short program with the other skaters.

After practice we learned some terrible news. Angela Nikodinov and her mother had been in a car accident on the way from the Portland airport. Angela was hurt, and her mom had passed away.

It was such a horrible surprise to everyone. I felt so sad because I knew Angela was really close to her mom. My thoughts and all my sympathy were with her and her family. And it gave me a real shock of perspective about the competition—it kind of brought all of us back to earth, a huge reminder that skating isn't everything.

And then it was Thursday, time to perform my short. I was a little tentative—it was the first time I'd performed my short program all year, and really my only big performance since the 2004 Worlds. I was still kind of getting my feet under me, and it was a real turning point in my season. But everything had finally come together—the dress, the program. I was happy with my performance and feeling a lot more confident by the end of the day.

Being at a competition with Mr. Nicks again felt great, familiar and comfortable. He kept joking that my practices were so good, it was making his job easy. We click well, and he's a good ally in a competitive situation—very mellow, very calm.

On Friday I had another practice, this time my long program, at Memorial Coliseum, and it went very smoothly. My practices were all solid, which was a really great feeling after such a difficult season. And after that there were more interviews, and then dinner with my mom.

For once, I didn't feel too nervous about the competition. Mostly it just felt great being back in a competition, the old routines of going to practices, putting on my makeup, doing my hair, getting ready, feeling the buzz of Nationals.

It's a wonderful event, with all the top skaters in the U.S. there, and everyone is so excited and supportive of each other. It was also great to see my friends and catch up with everyone I'd missed throughout the season. There's a special feeling at Nationals, with everyone together at one event. So I was really just glad to be back, and not thinking too much or getting too nervous about the long program.

✳ *Skating my short program at the 2005 Nationals*

Of course, I still had plenty of time to get nervous—I was scheduled to skate fifth on Saturday night, and there was a long time to wait. I walked around behind the curtain, staying warm, doing my usual precompetition stretches and trying to let loose and stay focused at the same time.

A few skaters before my turn, I went back to get changed, and then finally it was time to get on the ice.

The hesitation I'd felt going into the short program was gone. Now I felt aggressive, more excited than nervous. I pushed myself and didn't hold anything back. It was a great audience, and Nationals is always so packed with fans, media, cameras. It's thrilling, but I'm usually too jittery to enjoy it. So it was a nice change to feel the excitement and really have a good time on the ice.

I ended up making one major mistake, but I had absolutely no regrets. Being able to skate all out, to have fun with my program and really go for it, was all I'd wanted. There was no need to put my hand down on my triple loop; it was a silly mistake. And I was a little tired going into the Lutz and wasn't able to hang on to the landing. But overall I was really happy that I was able to come back strong and finish the program well.

In the kiss-and-cry area Mr. Nicks said to me, "Good job, you're getting there." We didn't say much else—we know each other so well, it was comfortable just to sit there with him, both of us knowing that I'd come such a long way since my struggles earlier in the season.

It was a satisfying competition for me, and a big turning point for all of us: It would be the last year that the old scoring system would be in place at Nationals.

Throughout the season the International Skating Union's new computerized system had been phased in, and starting with the 2005 Worlds, the new scoring, which would count every element and grade artistic expression

✳ *Me and Timmy with our silver medals*

✳ *2005 Nationals—finished with my long program*

more precisely, would go into effect permanently. I was excited to develop my program, adapting it to the new system. Even if it meant not getting a 6.0, the new scoring would also be more exact and a fairer arrangement for the skaters.

After the long programs were over it was time for the competitors' party, held at the main hotel. I got to see Tiffany Stiegler, who had skated really well in the pairs dance competition with Sergey Magerovskiy. And I had a chance to congratulate Johnny on his second Nationals win and Timmy on his silver medal. We had fun at the party, eating and talking and getting temporary tattoos (I got a black-and-red sun and a Chinese symbol on my back).

We didn't get much sleep that night, which made it hard to get up Sunday morning for exhibition practice. Plus I forgot my Worlds team photo dress at the hotel. I had to send my dad back to get it and change really quickly before the photo shoot.

For the exhibition I skated my *Romeo and Juliet* routine, which I hadn't done for an entire year. During the practice I was having a hard time remembering everything, and the performance was not one of my best.

We were supposed to fly home the next day, but suddenly I felt homesick and asked my mom if we could try to leave that night instead. We rushed back to the hotel, threw our stuff into our suitcases, and made it to the airport just in time for the last flight out. All the rushing was completely worth it, though, for the feeling of happiness and relief I felt when I woke up in my own bed the next morning.

Have I mentioned how nice it was to be back in California?

Now I had a month to get ready for the Worlds competition. I needed to work on my routine, getting it ready for the new scoring system and also making it sharper and cleaner and stronger.

It was thrilling to be part of the U.S. team again, to be skating better than I had all year, to have so much to look forward to in terms of improving my skating and developing as a competitor. We'd be going back to Russia for Worlds, and I knew it would be a fun trip for me.

In the meantime, I was back in California, enjoying sunny warm weather—even in the middle of January. It felt like everything had really fallen into place. And I couldn't wait to get back on the ice again.